JUMPERS

Also by Tom Stoppard

JUMPERS

Tom Stoppard

Grove Press
New York

Printed in the United States of America

Library of Congress Catalog Card Number 73-21011
ISBN 978-0-8021-6081-2
eISBN 978-0-8021-9538-8

Grove Press
an imprint of Grove Atlantic
154 West 14th Street
New York, NY 10011

Distributed by Publishers Group West

groveatlantic.com

23 24 25 26 27   10 9 8 7 6 5 4 3 2 1

For Miriam

AUTHOR'S NOTE

In preparing previous plays for publication I have tried with some difficulty to arrive at something called a 'definitive text', but I now believe that in the case of plays there is no such animal. Each production will throw up its own problems and very often the solution will lie in some minor change to the text, either in the dialogue or in the author's directions, or both. What follows is a basic version of *Jumpers*. The National Theatre production was mounted on a revolve stage and this fact alone was responsible for various small changes to the links between scenes. I have also included here the stage directions relating to the wall-sized television screen which the National Theatre was able to provide, but such a screen is not intended to be essential to the play's workability. I also shortened the play slightly in ways which are not shown here.

T.S.

POSTSCRIPT (February 1973): . . . And indeed, after some months' absence *Jumpers* returned to the National Theatre in a slightly altered form. This edition incorporates the changes because they seem to me an improvement on the original. The main alteration consists of having the screens placed round the bed for the *first* bedroom scene in Act Two, rather than for the final bedroom scene, with a consequent adjustment of the dialogue. This gives a better shape to the Act, and I gratefully record that for this idea, and for much else, I am indebted to Peter Wood whose insight and inventiveness were a crucial influence on *Jumpers* throughout rehearsals. The other most noticeable change is the disappearance of Scott from the Coda, a more difficult decision but I think on balance the right one; he added little and delayed much.

There are three playing areas, the STUDY, the BEDROOM, and the HALL. There is also a SCREEN, hopefully forming a backdrop to the whole stage. Film and slides are to be back-projected on to this Screen on a scale big enough to allow actors and furniture to mask the images without significantly obscuring them.

It is an essential requirement of the play that the Bedroom can be blacked out completely while the action continues elsewhere. Where this cannot be achieved by lighting alone, it might be an idea to put the Bedroom in a permanent gauze box; but raising and lowering a gauze screen is not encouraged. Another possibility, where the facility exists would be to put the Bedroom on a revolve.

For the purpose of the stage directions given hereafter, I am assuming the following layout.

The FRONT DOOR is Upstage Centre. The HALL is right-angled, a passage coming downstage from the Front Door to the footlights turning Stage Right along the front of the stage and disappearing into the wing at Downstage Right, where it leads to unseen Kitchen, Living Room, etc.

The STUDY occupies the whole area stage Left of the Hall and Front Door.

The BEDROOM occupies the rest of the stage, i.e., the area inside the reverse-L-shape of the Hall.

The apartment belongs to GEORGE, a Professor of Moral Philosophy married to a prematurely-retired musical-comedy actress of some renown, DOROTHY. The general standard of living suggested by the fla owes more, one would guess, to musical comedy than moral philosophy and this is especially true of the Bedroom which is lushly carpeted and includes among its furnishings a television set remotely-controlled by an electronic portable switch; a record player; two elegant straight-backed chairs and one comfortable upholstered chair; a globular gold-fishbowl containing one goldfish; and a four-poster bed which can be enclosed at will by the drapes adorning its corners. The effect is elegant, feminine, expensive. The Bedroom has two doors, one leading into the wings at Stage Left (the unseen Bathroom), and the second into the Hall. This latter door must be sturdily fixed. It opens inwards, the hinges upstage, so that when this door is wide open the inside of it is hidden from the audience. The room also has a french window, guarded on the exterior by a mock-balcony or balustrade; it overlooks streets and sky, for the flat is in an upper floor of big old-fashioned but newly redecorated and converted mansion.

The STUDY *contains a day-bed against the upstage wall, bookshelves above the bed, a desk and chair for the Secretary, and a bigger desk for George placed against the footlights. On the wings-side of the room is a tall cupboard or wardrobe, and a small wash-basin with mirror. The room contains, somewhere, a tape-recorder; a bow and quiver of arrows, together with an archery target about a yard in diameter; an electric typewriter for the Secretary to use; a smallish wooden box such as a small tortoise might live in, and a large wooden box such as a rabbit might live in. There is a door into the Hall. The window would be in the fourth wall, but not above the desk for that space is occupied by a large (though imaginary) mirror. George's desk, when we discover it, is a clutter of books and manuscript, and a tumbler containing pencils.*

However, none of the above is visible for the first few minutes of the play, for which is required an empty space. . . .

JUMPERS

PRODUCTION CREDITS

Jumpers was first performed by the National Theatre Company at the Old Vic Theatre, London, on 2 February 1972.

The cast was as follows:

George	Michael Hordern
Dorothy	Diana Rigg
Archie	Graham Crowden
Bones	David Ryall
Crouch	Paul Curran
Secretary	Anna Carteret
Jumpers, etc.	Ray Callaghan
	Tom Dickinson
	Michael Edgar
	Tom Georgeson
	Lionel Guyett
	William Hobbs
	David Howey
	Barry James
	Brian Jameson
	Desmond McNamara
	Riggs O'Hara
	Howard Southern
	Harry Waters
Director	Peter Wood
Designer	Patrick Robertson

Jumpers opened in New York on 22 April 1974 at the Billy Rose Theatre.

The cast was as follows:

George	Brian Bedford
Dorothy	Jill Clayburgh
Archie	Remak Ramsay
Bones	Ronald Drake
Crouch	Walter Flanagan
Secretary	Joan Byron
Duncan McFee	Robert Rhys
Clegthorpe	William Rhys
Jumpers, etc.	Larry G. Bailey
	Larry Breeding
	Mark Hanks
	Bobby Lee
	Jim Litten
	Eddie Mekka
	Ross Miles
	Dale Muchmore
	Stan Picus
	George Ramos
	Jason Roberts
	Russell Robertson
	Gordon Joseph Weiss
Director	Peter Wood
Designer	Josef Svoboda
Lighting	Gilbert V. Hemsley, Jr.

4

A revival of *Jumpers* opened on Broadway at the Brooks Atkinson Theatre on 19 June 2003.

The cast was as follows:

George	Simon Russell Beale
Dorothy	Essie Davis
Archie	Nicky Henson
Bones	Nicholas Woodeson
Crouch	John Rogan
Secretary	Eliza Lumley
Jumpers, etc.	Michael Arnold
	Andrew Asnes
	Clark Scott Carmichael
	Tom Hildebrand
	Michael Hollick (Greystoke)
	Don Johanson
	Joseph P. McDonnell
	Hillel Meltzer (McFee)
Director	David Leveaux
Designer	Vicki Mortimer
Lighting	Paule Constable

CHARACTERS

George is between 40 and 50, and still attractive enough to make it perfectly plausible that he should be married to Dotty who is ten to fifteen years younger and very beautiful indeed.

Archie is a dandy, as old as George or older.

Inspector Bones is middle-aged and carelessly dressed.

Crouch is old and small and a bit stooped.

The Secretary is young and attractive but poker-faced, almost grim, even on her first appearance, in which she performs as a stripper.

The Jumpers are dressed in yellow uniforms—tracksuit trousers and singlets and although they pass muster at first glance, they are not as universally youthful or athletic-looking as one might expect.

ACT ONE

ARCHIE (*unseen*)   And now, ladies and gentlemen, on the occasion of a momentous victory at the polls, may I present your hostess and mine, making a most welcome reappearance, the much-missed, much-loved star of the musical stage, the incomparable, magnetic Dorothy Moore!

DOTTY *enters. Much applause.*

ᴅᴏᴛᴛʏ   Thank you, thank you for coming.

Music introduction for 'Shine On Harvest Moon'. She dries.

And now, making a most welcome reappearance, the incomparable, unreliable, neurotic Dorothy Moore.

Applause. Cheers. Introduction repeated.

How does it begin?

GUESTS, *offstage, sing* 'Shine on, shine on harvest moon'. *Singing, but going wrong immediately.*

I want to spoon to my honey I'll croon love's June or July. (*Breaks off.*) No I can't. I'm sorry (*and goes*).

Drum roll.

Cries of disappointment change to cries of delight.

Like a pendulum between darkness and darkness, the SECRETARY *swings into the spotlight, and out. She is on a swing, making an arc from wing to wing, in sight for a second, out of sight for a second, in sight for a second, out of sight for a second . . . back and forth. The swing itself hangs from a chandelier.*

9

Cheers.

Each time she reappears she has taken off some clothing.

Grateful cheers.

CROUCH *enters from side, the porter pressed into service to serve drinks at the party. He wears a short white coat and carries a round tray balanced on one hand, drinks on tray.*

He is going to stray into the line of vision. Voices warn him away, good-humouredly.

Crouch does not know what is going on: every time he turns downstage, the Secretary is in view behind him, and every time he looks upstage the gap is empty.

'Mind your back!'
'Out the way!'
'Let the dog see the rabbit!'

Crouch is bewildered.

The Secretary is nearing nakedness, obscured. The unseen watchers are nearing hysterical frustration.

At the climax of their cries, Crouch backs into the path of the swing and is knocked arse over tip by a naked lady, BLACKOUT *and crash of broken glass. Immediately:*

ARCHIE (*voice only*)   'And now!—ladies and gentlemen!—the INCREDIBLE—RADICAL!—LIBERAL!!—JUMPERS!!'

White spot. Musical introduction.

EIGHT JUMPERS *enter jumping, tumbling, somersaulting, four from each side of the stage: a not especially talented troupe of gymnasts possibly using a trampoline.*

Discreet musical accompaniment.

Their separate entrances converge to form a tableau of modest pretension.

10

DOTTY (*entering*)   That's not incredible. . . . Well, is it? I can sing better than that. I mean I can sing better than they can jump.

Dotty wanders on to the stage in front of the now disassembling tableau. Her blonde hair is elegantly 'up', her white dress is long and billowy . . . she looks fabulous, stunning. She flaps a hand dismissively at the Jumpers.

(*Equably.*) No good—you're still credible. (*Generally.*) Get me someone unbelievable!

GEORGE, *holding sheets of paper, has already entered behind her, and as Dotty turns on her last word she is face to face with him, and continues without pause.*

Promptness I like.

George is not dressed for a party. Flannels and shabby smoking jacket, hair awry, his expression and manner signifying remonstrance. The Jumpers persevere, doggedly helping each other to do back-flips, etc.

I have a complaint. These people are supposed to be incredible and I'm not even astonished. I am not faintly surprised. In fact, not only can I sing better than they can jump, I can probably jump higher than they can sing.

GEORGE   For God's sake. It's after two a.m.

She turns to the presumed source of music.

DOTTY   Give me a C.

George goes as far as to touch her arm. She turns on him with sudden obliterating fury.

It's my bloody party, George!

George leaves.

A Jumper flips himself into a standing position in mid-stage.

(*Equable again.*) I can do that.

11

A second Jumper joins the first.

And that.

A third Jumper leaps on to the shoulders of the first two.

I can't do that, but my belief is unshakeable, so get off.
(*To the unseen musicians.*) I'll do the one about the moon.
I'm sure you know it.

> *A word about Dotty's Song. The musicians attempt to follow her but are thwarted by her inability to distinguish between one moon-song and another, and by her habit of singing the words of one to the tune of another. The music gamely keeps switching tracks, but Dotty keeps double-crossing it.*

(*Sings.*) Shine on, shine on, harvest moon
I want to spoon
To my honey I'll croon love's June
Or July——
—No, that's not it——
(*Sings.*) Shine on, shine on silvery moon
I used to sigh
In June or July
How high the——
—No, you've gone wrong again——
(*Sings.*) moon, you saw me standing alone——

> *The last six words have fortuitously combined the words and tune of 'Blue Moon'.*

That's it, that's it!

> *Now confident, she starts to play the* chanteuse, *strolling in and out among the dogged Jumpers, moving upstage of them and turning.*

(*Sings.*) Blue moon
You saw me standing alone
Without a dream in my heart
It must have been moonglow

Way up in the Blue Moon
You saw me standing——
No, no——

Shouts at Jumpers.

All right, I believe you!—you're incredible! And now for another song.

From now until their act is terminated by events, the Jumpers are assembling themselves into a human pyramid composed thus: Six Jumpers in three-two-one formation, flanked by the other two standing on their hands at the pyramid's base. When the pyramid is complete it hides Dotty from view.

(*Sings.*) You saw me standing in June
January, Allegheny, Moon or July—
(*Jeers.*) Jumpers I've had—yellow, I've had them all! *Incredible, barely* credible, credible and all too bloody likely——When I say jump, *jump!*

From her tone now it should be apparent that Dotty, who may have appeared pleasantly drunk, is actually breaking up mentally. And from her position in the near-dark outside the Jumpers' light, it should be possible to believe that Dotty is responsible for what happens next— which is:

A gun shot.

One Jumper, bottom row, second from left, is blown out of the pyramid. He falls downstage, leaving the rest of the pyramid intact. The music has stopped.

Dotty, chanteuse, walks through the gap in the pyramid.

The shot Jumper is at her feet. He starts to move, dying, pulling himself up against Dotty's legs. She looks at him in surprise as he crawls up her body. His blood is on her dress. She holds him under his arms, and looks around in a bewildered way. She whimpers.

Archie. . . .

The pyramid has been defying gravity for these few seconds. Now it slowly collapses into the dark, imploding on the missing part, and rolling and separating, out of sight, leaving only the white spot.

Dotty does not move, holding the Jumper.

ARCHIE (*voice only*)   . . .
(*The Party hubbub comes back, at a higher pitch.*) Quiet please. . . .
The party is over . . .

A DRUNK (*sings*)   It's time to call it a day . . .

This sets off a ripple of applause and cheers.

The party noise dies to silence.

The light contracts to a spot on Dotty and the Jumper, eerily. Frozen time, Dotty still has not moved.

DOTTY   Archie . . .

ARCHIE (*off*)   Oh dear!

DOTTY   Archie . . .

ARCHIE (*off*)   Just keep him out of sight till morning. I'll be back.

DOTTY   Archie . . .

ARCHIE (*off*)   Hush . . . I'll be back at eight o'clock.

Around her, the flat assembles itself, Bedroom, Study, Hall.

The white spot remains—on the Screen now: but it is changing in character, and becomes a map of the moon photographed from a satellite . . . the familiar pitted circle. At the same time is heard the low tone of the TELEVISION VOICE, too low to admit comprehension. The picture changes to a close up of the moon's surface.

We are watching a television programme about something that has happened on the moon.

The picture changes several times—an astronaut, a rocket, a moon-vehicle, etc.

The television set in the Bedroom is on.

Dotty is standing in the Bedroom. She hasn't moved at all. She is dressed in a blood-stained party frock, holding up a corpse dressed in yellow trousers and singlet. She is composed, looking about her, clearly trying to decide what to do with the body.

In the Study, George is working at the desk, adding to a pile of manuscript.

The Front Door opens, Crouch enters, using a master key. He is not wearing the white coat now, but a grey overall as worn by janitors. He is limping slightly. He is singing quietly to himself . . . 'Gonna make a sentimental journey . . . gonna put my heart at ease . . . gonna take a sentimental journey . . .'

Dotty has heard him. She turns down the sound of the TV, using the remote control device.

DOTTY   Darling! . . .

CROUCH   It's Crouch, Madam.

Crouch continues and exits to Kitchen.

Dotty sits down on the bed, the corpse slumped over her knees. She glances at the TV. She turns up the volume.

TV VOICE   —in a tight spot. And so in the crippled space capsule, Captain Scott is on his way back to earth, the first Englishman to reach the moon, but his triumph will be overshadowed by the memory of Astronaut Oates, a tiny receding figure waving forlornly from the featureless wastes of the lunar landscape.

Dotty changes the channel.

On the Screen: a big Procession in the streets of London, military in tone (brass band music) but celebratory: for five seconds.

Dotty changes the channel.

A commercial: for three seconds.

15

Dotty changes the channel.

The Moon Programme again.

—which followed the discovery that the damage on impact had severely reduced the thrust of the rockets that are fired for take-off. Millions of viewers saw the two astronauts struggling at the foot of the ladder until Oates was knocked to the ground by his commanding officer. . . . Captain Scott has maintained radio silence since pulling up the ladder and closing the hatch with the remark, 'I am going up now. I may be gone for some time.'

Dotty changes channel. The Procession on Screen. Military music. She looks gloomily, helplessly at the corpse. She notes the blood on her dress. She takes the dress off.

Crouch enters from the Kitchen, carrying a bin of rubbish and several empty champagne bottles.

Dotty hears the kitchen door. She turns the TV sound down low.

DOTTY What time is it, Crouch?

CROUCH Nearly nine o'clock, Madam.

Crouch leaves by the Front Door as the Secretary enters. The Secretary hurries in, in the act of taking off her overcoat and hat.

Crouch lets himself out, closing the Front Door. The Secretary enters the Study, closes the door behind her, hangs up her hat and coat on a hook on the downstage side of the wardrobe, sits down at her desk, and arranges her notebook and pencil. George has continued to write without looking up.

DOTTY (*very quietly*) Help! (*Slightly louder.*) Help!

George looks up and stares thoughtfully at the audience (into the mirror). He looks down again and continues to write.

The Bedroom BLACKS OUT.

George stops writing, gets to his feet. His system—for preparing lectures—is to scrawl them over many pieces of paper, which he then dictates to the Secretary who will type them out. In dictating, George prefers to address the large mirror in the fourth wall. He does not take much notice of the Secretary.

George now collects the pages into a tidy sheaf, takes a pace back from the mirror, assumes a suitable stance, and takes it from the top. . . .

GEORGE Secondly! . . .

He has ambushed himself. He looks around and retrieves the missing sheet from behind his desk.

DOTTY (*off*) Help!

George takes up his stance anew.

GEORGE To begin at the beginning ——

DOTTY (*off. Panic*) Help! Murder!

George throws his manuscript on to the desk and marches angrily to the door.

(*Off.*) Oh, horror, horror, horror! Confusion now hath made its masterpiece . . . most sacrilegious murder!——(*Different voice.*) Woe, alas! What, in our house?

George, with his hand on the door handle, pauses. He returns to his desk and picks up his papers.

GEORGE To begin at the beginning: is God? (*Pause.*) I prefer to put the question in this form because to ask, 'Does God exist?' appears to presuppose the existence of a God who may not, and I do not propose this late evening to follow my friend Russell, this evening to follow my late friend Russell, to follow my good friend the late Lord Russell, necrophiliac rubbish!, to begin at the beginning: is God? (*He ponders a moment.*) To ask, 'Is God?' appears to presuppose a Being who perhaps isn't . . . and thus is open to the same objection as the question, 'Does God exist?' . . . but until

17

the difficulty is pointed out it does not have the same propensity to confuse language with meaning and to conjure up a God who may have any number of predicates including omniscience, perfection and four-wheel-drive but not, as it happens, existence. This confusion, which indicates only that language is an approximation of meaning and not a logical symbolism for it, began with Plato and was not ended by Bertrand Russell's theory that existence could only be asserted of descriptions and not of individuals, but I do not propose this evening to follow into the Theory of Descriptions my very old friend—now dead, of course—*ach!*—to follow into the Theory of Descriptions, the late Lord Russell———!

—if I may so refer to an old friend for whom punctuality was no less a predicate than existence, and a good deal more so, he would have had us believe, though why we should believe that existence could be asserted of the author of *Principia Mathematica* but not of Bertrand Russell, he never had time, despite his punctuality, not to mention his existence, to explain, very good, keep to the point, to begin at the beginning: *is God?* (*To Secretary.*) Leave a space. Secondly! A small number of men, by the exercise of their intellects and by the study of the works both of nature and of other intellects before them, have been able to argue coherently against the existence of God. A much larger number of men, by the exercise of their emotional and psychological states, have affirmed that this is the correct view. This view derives partly from what is known as common sense, whose virtue, uniquely among virtues, is that everybody has it, and partly from the mounting implausibility of a technological age as having divine origins—for while a man might believe that the providence of sheep's wool was made in heaven, he finds it harder to believe the same of Terylene mixture. (*He leans into the mirror intently.*) Well, the tide is running his way, and it is a tide which has turned only once in human history. . . . There is presumably a calendar date—a *moment*—when the onus of proof passed from the atheist to the believer, when, quite suddenly, secretly, the noes had it. (*And squeezes a blackhead in the imaginary mirror. Then he straightens up and is the lecturer again.*) It is now nearly fifty years since Professor Ramsay described theology and ethics as two subjects without an object, and yet, as though to defy reason, as though to flaunt a divine indestructibility, the question will not go away: is God?

DOTTY (*off*) Rape!

GEORGE And then again, I sometimes wonder whether the question ought not to be, 'Are God?' Because it is to account for two quite unconnected mysteries that the human mind looks beyond humanity and it is two of him that philosophy obligingly provides. There is, first, the God of Creation to account for existence, and, second, the God of Goodness to account for moral values. I say they are unconnected because there is no logical reason why the fountainhead of goodness in the universe should have necessarily created the universe in the first place; nor is it necessary, on the other hand, that a Creator should care tuppence about the behaviour of his creations. Still, at least in the Judaeo–Christian tradition, nothing is heard either of a God who created the universe and then washed his hands of it, or, alternatively, a God who merely took a comparatively recent interest in the chance product of universal gases. In practice, people admit a Creator to give authority to moral values, and admit moral values to give point to the Creation. But when we place the existence of God within the discipline of a philosophical inquiry, we find these two independent mysteries: the how and the why of the overwhelming question:——

DOTTY (*off*) *Is anybody there?*

GEORGE (*pause*) Perhaps all mystical experience is a form of coincidence. Or vice versa, of course.

Dotty screams. It sounds in earnest. Of course, nothing can be seen.

(*Murmurs.*) Wolf. . . .

DOTTY (*off*) Wolves!—Look out!

George throws his manuscript down furiously.

19

(*Off.*) Murder—Rape—Wolves!

George opens his door and shouts at the enclosed Bedroom door.

GEORGE Dorothy, I will not have my work interrupted by these gratuitous acts of lupine delinquency!

The Procession Music, which had been allowed to fade out, is brought up by the opening of the Study door.

And turn that thing down!—you are deliberately feigning an interest in brass band music to distract me from my lecture! (*He closes his door, and from behind it produces a quiver of arrows and a bow. These he brings downstage and places them on his desk.*)

(*Pleasantly.*) Does, for the sake of argument, God, so to speak, exist?

He returns upstage and finds an archery target, which he leans up against the upstage bookcase, resting on the day-bed.

(*To mirror.*) My method of inquiry this evening into certain aspects of this hardy perennial may strike some of you as overly engaging, but experience has taught me that to attempt to sustain the attention of rival schools of academics by argument alone is tantamount to constructing a Gothic arch out of junket.

He extracts an arrow from the quiver.

Putting aside the God of Goodness, to whom we will return, and taking first the God of Creation—or to give him his chief philosophical *raison d'être*, the First Cause—we see that a supernatural or divine origin is the logical consequence of the assumption that one thing leads to another, and that this series must have had a first term; that, if you like, though chickens and eggs may alternate back through the millennia, ultimately, we arrive at something which, while perhaps no longer resembling either a chicken or an egg, is nevertheless the first term of that series and can itself only be attributed to a First Cause—or to give it its theological soubriquet, God. How well founded is such an assumption? Could it be, for instance, that chickens and eggs have been succeeding each other in one form or another literally for ever? My old friend—Mathematicians are quick to point out that they are familiar with many series which have no first term— such as the series of proper fractions between nought and one. What, they ask is the first, that is the smallest, of these fractions? A billionth? A trillionth? Obviously not: Cantor's proof that there is no greatest number ensures that there is no smallest fraction. There is no beginning. (*With a certain relish he notches his arrow into the bowstring.*) But it was precisely this notion of infinite series which in the sixth century BC led the Greek philosopher Zeno to conclude that since an arrow shot towards a target first had to cover half the distance, and then half the remainder, and then half the remainder after that, and so on *ad infinitum*, the result was, as I will now demonstrate, that though an arrow is always approaching its target, it never quite gets there, and Saint Sebastian died of fright.

He is about to fire the arrow, but changes his mind, and turns back to the mirror.

Furthermore, by a similar argument he showed that *before* reaching the half-way point, the arrow had to reach the quarter mark, and before that the eighth, and before that the sixteenth, and so on, with the result, remembering Cantor's proof, that the arrow *could not move at all!*

DOTTY (*off*) *Fire!*

George fires, startled before he was ready, and the arrow disappears over the top of the wardrobe.

Help—rescue—fire!

GEORGE (*shouts furiously*) Will you stop this childish nonsense! Thanks to you I have lost the element of surprise!

He tosses the bow away, tries to peer on tiptoe over the wardrobe, which is too high, and desists. He picks up his script, and then puts it down again, and sits on the corner of his desk, one leg swinging, arms folded. He notices that his socks do not match. The Secretary, unruffled, waits patiently, her pencil is poised. (It may as well be stated now that she never speaks.)

(*Subdued at first.*) Look. . . . Consider my left sock. My left sock exists but it need not have done so. It is, we say, not necessary, but contingent. Why does my sock exist? Because a sock–maker made it, in one sense; because, in another, at some point previously, the conception of a sock arrived in the human brain; to keep my foot warm in a third, to make a profit in a fourth. There is reason and there is cause and there is the question, who made the sock-maker's maker? etcetera, very well, next! see, see, I move my foot which moves my sock. (Walks.) I and my foot and my sock all move round the room, which moves round the sun, which also moves, as Aristotle said, though not round the earth, he was wrong about that. There is reason and there is cause and there is motion, each in infinite regress towards a moment of origin and a point of ultimate reference—and one day!—as we stare into the fire at the mouth of our cave, suddenly! in an instant of grateful terror, we get it!—the one and only, sufficient unto himself, outside the action, uniquely immobile!—the Necessary Being, the First Cause, the Unmoved Mover!!

He takes a climactic drink from his tumbler, which however contains only pencils. He puts the tumbler down, leaving a pencil in his mouth.

(*Indistinctly.*) St. Thomas Aquinas. . . .

He drops the pencil back into the tumbler.

(*Quietly.*) Of the five proofs of God's existence put forward by St. Thomas Aquinas, three depended on the simple idea that if an apparently endless line of dominoes is knocking itself over one by one then somewhere there is a domino which was *nudged*. And as regards dominoes, I haven't got any further than St. Thomas.

The music from the TV Procession has been quietly reestablishing itself in the background.

Everything has to begin somewhere and there is no answer to *that*. Except, of course, why does it? Why, since we accept the notion of

22

infinity without end, should we not accept the logically identical notion of infinity without beginning? My old——Consider the series of proper fractions. Etcetera. (*To Secretary.*) Then Cantor, then no beginning, etcetera, then Zeno. Insert: But the fact is, the first term of the series is not an infinite fraction but *zero*. It exists. God, so to speak, is nought. Interesting. Continue.

By missing the point of a converging series Zeno overlooked the fallacy which is exemplified at its most picturesque in his famous paradoxes, which showed in every way but experience that an arrow could never reach its target, and that a tortoise given a head start in a race with, say, a hare, could never be overtaken—and by way of regaining your attention I will now demonstrate the nature of that fallacy; to which end I have brought with me a specially trained tortoise—(*which he takes from the smaller wooden box*)—and a similarly trained, damn and blast!—— (*He has opened the larger box and found it empty. He looks round.*)

Thumper! Thumper, where are you, boy?

Failing to find Thumper under the desks or the bed, he leaves the room and, carrying the tortoise, enters the Bedroom, opening the door wide and leaving it open as the Bedroom lights up. Procession on Screen. Procession music loud now, as though we travelled with him. The body of the Jumper is nowhere in sight. However, Dotty's nude body is sprawled face down, and apparently lifeless on the bed. George takes in the room at a glance, ignores Dotty, and still calling for Thumper goes to look in the bathroom.

George reappears from the Bathroom after a second or two. Mixed in with the TV music now is a snatch of commentary.

TV VOICE   . . . beautiful blue sky for the fly-past, and here they come!

Very loud: the jet planes scream and thunder on the sound track and scream and thunder across the Screen. In mid-flight they are cut off. George has turned off the TV: silence and white Screen, George still moving towards the door, from the bed where the TV switch is lying.

GEORGE   Are you a proverb?

DOTTY   No, I'm a book.

GEORGE   *The Naked and the Dead.*

DOTTY   Stay with me!

The four lines have been rapid. George is now at the door, ready to leave. Dotty has sat up on the bed.

DOTTY   Play with me . . .

GEORGE (*hesitating*)   Now . . . ?

DOTTY   I mean *games*——

George makes to leave.

Be nice. (*George moves. Desperate.*) I'll let you!

*George leaves, shutting the door and thus revealing the corpse to the audience. He re-enters, and the corpse is obscured again.**

GEORGE   Do I say 'My friend the late Bertrand Russell' or 'My late friend Bertrand Russell'? They both sound funny. (*Pause.*)

DOTTY   Probably because he wasn't your friend.

GEORGE   Well, I don't know about that.

DOTTY (*angrily*)   He was *my* friend. If he hadn't asked me who was that bloke always hanging about, you'd never have met him.

GEORGE   Nevertheless, I did meet him, and we talked animatedly for some time.

DOTTY   As I recall, *you* talked animatedly for some time about language being the aniseed trail that draws the hounds of heaven when the metaphysical fox has gone to earth; he must have thought you were barmy.

---

* In the event, the corpse was not hung on the back of the Bedroom door, in the original production, but on the inside of the door of a cupboard adjacent to the Bedroom door; the closing of the Bedroom door mysteriously caused the opening of the cupboard door, a device gratefully borrowed from the famous Robert Dhery sketch in *La Plume de ma Tante.*

GEORGE (*hurt*)   I resent that. My metaphor of the fox and the hounds was an allusion, as Russell well understood, to his Theory of Descriptions.

DOTTY   The Theory of Descriptions was not what was on his mind that night. For one thing it was sixty years since he'd thought it up, and for another he was trying to telephone Mao Tse Tung.

GEORGE   I was simply trying to bring his mind back to matters of universal import, and away from the day-to-day parochialism of international politics.

DOTTY   *Universal import!* You're living in dreamland!

GEORGE   Oh really? Well, I wouldn't have thought that trying to get the local exchange to put you through to Chairman Mao with the wine-waiter from the Pagoda Garden hanging on to the bedroom extension to interpret, showed a grasp of the real world. (*He goes to leave.*) Thumper! Where are you, Thumper?

DOTTY   Georgie!—I'll let you.

He halts.

GEORGE   I don't want to be 'let'. Can't you see that it's an insult?

Dotty drops back on to the bed in a real despair, and perhaps a real contrition.

DOTTY   Oh God . . . if only Archie would come.

GEORGE (*coldly*)   Is he coming *again*?

DOTTY   I don't know. Do you mind?

GEORGE   Well, he's dropped in to see you every day this week. What am I supposed to think?

DOTTY   I don't believe I like your tone.

GEORGE   I have no tone. But I would like tonelessly to make the point that if he intends to visit you on a regular basis then either he

25

should come after lunch or you should get up before it. Receiving in the bedroom is liable to get a woman talked about, unless it is an authentic salon.

DOTTY How dare you?—Go on, get out and write your stupid speech for your dreamland debating society! I thought for once—I mean I seriously thought I might get a little—understanding—yes, finding myself in a bit of a spot, I seriously considered trusting you—for a little panache, without a lot of pedantic questions and hadn't-we-better-inform-the-authorities, I mean we should be able to rise *above* that—but not *you*, oh no, do you wonder I turn to Archie——?

She lies down on the bed and pulls the cover over her.

GEORGE (*reckless, committed*) I can put two and two together, you know. Putting two and two together is my *subject*. I do not leap to hasty conclusions. I do not deal in suspicion and wild surmise. I examine the data; I look for logical inferences. We have on the one hand, that is to say in bed, an attractive married woman whose relationship with her husband stops short only of the issue of a ration book; we have on the other hand daily visits by a celebrated ladies' man who rings the doorbell, is admitted by Mrs. Thing who shows him into the bedroom, whence he emerges an hour later looking more than a little complacent and crying, 'Don't worry, I'll let myself out!'

He lapses into a calm suavity.

Now let us see. What can we make of it all? Wife in bed, daily visits by gentlemen caller. Does anything suggest itself?

DOTTY (*calmly*) Sounds to me he's the doctor.

George is staggered.

GEORGE (*pause*) Doctor? . . . The Vice-Chancellor?

DOTTY (*spiritedly*) You *know* he's a bloody doctor!

26

GEORGE   I know he's a qualified psychiatrist, but he doesn't practise. I mean he isn't a chap who goes around looking down people's *throats*. His line is psychotics . . . manic depressives—schizos—fantasisers——

Dotty picks up her mirror and starts brushing her hair.

(*Catching up.*) You mean you're bad again? (*Pause.*) I'm sorry. . . . How was I supposed to know you were . . .

DOTTY   I'm all right in here.

Pause.

GEORGE   Why did he bring you flowers? Not that there's any reason, of course, why he shouldn't bring you flowers.

DOTTY   Quite.

GEORGE   I mean, he's our friend, more or less. He likes you. Do you like him?

DOTTY   He's all right in his way.

GEORGE   What way is that?

DOTTY   Oh, you know.

GEORGE   No. What does he do?

DOTTY   He's a doctor.

Pause.

He keeps my spirits up.

GEORGE   Does he? That's . . . good.

DOTTY   I won't see him any more, if you like. (*Turns to him.*) I'll see you. If you like.

George examines the new tone, and decides the moment is genuine.

GEORGE (*softening*)   Oh, Dotty. . . . The first day you walked into my class . . . I thought, '*That's* better!' . . . It was a wet day . . . your

27

hair was wet . . . and I thought, 'The hyacinth girl' . . . and 'How my hair is growing thin'.

DOTTY   And I thought, 'I'll sit quiet and they won't find out I'm stupid' . . . and 'What a modest way with lovely words', and 'How his hair is growing thin'.

GEORGE   And you started to sit nearer the front.

DOTTY   You didn't look any younger.

GEORGE (*pang*)   And then you fell among theatricals.

DOTTY   But it was still all right.

GEORGE   Oh yes, for a time. And then again, it wasn't. And then again, it sometimes is, even now, when all else fails you.

DOTTY (*going to him*)   George, I'm in a bit of a spot.

GEORGE   What?

DOTTY (*touching him*)   Promise not to be stuffy.

GEORGE (*responding to the touch*)   We'll be unstuffy together . . . if you like.

DOTTY (*touching his face*)   You haven't shaved. You look awful.

GEORGE   I'll shave then . . . if you like.

DOTTY   All right . . . I feel a bit starved.

GEORGE   So do I.

DOTTY   Food, I meant . . .

GEORGE   Afterwards.

DOTTY   Before.

GEORGE (*moving away*)   On second thoughts . . .

DOTTY   Haven't you invented God *yet*?

GEORGE   Nearly; I'm having him typed out.

She restrains him from leaving.

DOTTY   Please. . . . Shave.

GEORGE (*pause*)   All right.

The jets come back, screaming over the house. George stares out of the french window. Dotty looks up at the ceiling.

A parade!

DOTTY   A parade!

GEORGE   Oh yes, the Radical Liberals. . . . It seems in dubious taste. . . . Soldiers . . . fighter planes. . . . After all, it was a general election, not a *coup d'état*.

DOTTY   It's funny you should say that.

GEORGE   Why?

DOTTY   Archie says it was a *coup d'état* not a general election.

GEORGE   Glib nonsense. It is unthinkable that the Radical Liberal Party could manipulate the democratic process.

DOTTY   Democracy is all in the head.

GEORGE   And anyway, you can't get away with that sort of thing. Everything comes out in the wash, sooner or later.

DOTTY   Then God help me and the Government.

GEORGE   Furthermore, I had a vote.

DOTTY   It's not the voting that's democracy, it's the counting, Archie says.

GEORGE (*angrily*)   Archie this, Archie that! Just for today I don't want to know anything about anything remotely to do with Archie! (*He moves away.*) I'm going to shave.

DOTTY   You may as well grow a beard.

GEORGE (*to the goldfish*)   Good morning! (*to Dotty*) His water needs changing.

George disappears into the Bathroom but reappears almost immediately, with a can of shaving foam. He applies the foam to his face, giving himself a white beard.

What did you mean, God help you and the Government?

DOTTY (*suddenly merry and mischievous*)   I only mentioned God reflexively (*and sees him*), old man, not as a true invocation.

GEORGE (*with asperity*)   Whenever you are like this I always think how unjust it is that so many people must have looked at us and said, 'What on earth made *her* marry *him*?'

He disappears back into the Bathroom.

DOTTY (*still merry*)   And yet, Professor, one can't help wondering at the persistence of the reflex, the universal constant unthinking appeal to the non-existent God who is presumed dead. Perhaps he's only missing in action, shot down behind the thin yellow lines of advancing Rad-Libs and getting himself together to go BOO!

He returns holding his razor.

GEORGE   Have you been shaving your legs?

DOTTY   And so our tutorials descended, from the metaphysical to the merely physical . . . not so much down to earth as down to the carpet, do you remember?

New tone. George, half foamed, bibbed, sits on the bed.

That was the year of 'The Concept of Knowledge', your masterpiece, and the last decent title left after Ryle bagged 'The Concept of Mind' and Archie bagged 'The Problem of Mind' and Ayer bagged 'The Problem of Knowledge'—and 'The Concept of Knowledge' might have made you if you had written it, but we were still on the carpet when an American with an Italian name working in Melbourne bagged it for a rather bad book which sold four copies in London, three to unknown purchasers and the fourth to yourself. He'd stolen a march while you were still comparing knowledge in the sense of having-experience-of, with knowledge in the sense of being-acquainted-with, and knowledge in the sense of inferring facts with knowledge in the sense of comprehending truths, and all the time as you got more and more acquainted with, though no more comprehending of, the symbolic patterns on my Persian carpet, it was knowing in the biblical sense of screwing that you were learning about and maybe there's a book in you yet——

George throws down his bib.

—or did you mean about me and the government?

As she crosses to pick up the goldfish bowl. George stops and turns, with dignity.

GEORGE   I don't believe you know anything about it. You are the wife of an academic: that means you are twice removed from the centre of events.

DOTTY   Archie says that the academics can look forward to rather more radicalism than liberalism.

She takes the goldfish bowl into the Bathroom.

GEORGE (*carefully reassuring himself*)   Radicalism has a fine and honourable tradition in this country. It will always involve a healthy scepticism about inherited means and ends, that is all.

Dotty re-enters with the goldfish bowl, emptied and upside down, over her head. She walks with the leaden-footed gait of a moon-walker, George ignores her.

I mean, it would be presumptuous to condemn radical ideas simply because they appear to me to be self-evidently stupid and criminal if they do happen to be at the same time radical, (*Dotty, moonwalking, affects to find and stoop for a small coin, which she holds up for George, who does not pause.*) 'The Moon and Sixpence'.

It is, after all, a radical idea to ensure freedom of the individual by denying it to groups.

Dotty takes off the fish bowl and replaces it on its table, somewhat pointlessly now.

Indeed, any party which calls itself radical might be said to have forfeited this claim if it *neglected* to take over the broadcasting services and send the Church Commissioners to prison——

DOTTY   It wasn't the Church Commissioners, it was property companies and Masters of Foxhounds.

GEORGE   I thought the Church Commissioners *were* a property company.

DOTTY   They were dispossessed, retroactively, as a humane gesture.

She tosses him a Times *newspaper from the table beside the bed.*

GEORGE   Well, what about the Church Commissioners who were also Masters of Foxhounds?

DOTTY   *I* don't know—Darling, I'm starving—

GEORGE *(turns a page. Morosely)*   There's a photograph here of the Association of National Newspaper Proprietors sitting in the back of a police car with a raincoat over their heads.

DOTTY   At least it's a government which keeps its promises.

GEORGE *(flinging down the paper)*   This isn't political theory! To think that these simplistic score-settlers should have appropriated the battle-scarred colours of those true radicals who fought for universal suffrage and the repeal of the Corn Laws——! *(Raving.)* And how is the Church to pay its clergy? Are they going to pull down the churches?

DOTTY   Yes. *(He gapes.)* The Church is going to be rationalized.

GEORGE   *Rationalized?* *(Furiously.)* You can't rationalize the Thirty-Nine Articles!

DOTTY   No, no . . . not the faith, the fabric. You remember how they rationalized the railways?—well, now they're going to rationalize the Church. (*Pause.*) There was an announcement on television.

GEORGE   Who by?

DOTTY   The Archbishop of Canterbury. Clegthorpe.

GEORGE   *Clegthorpe? Sam Clegthorpe?*

DOTTY   It's been made a political appointment, like judges.

GEORGE   Are you telling me that the Radical Liberal spokesman for Agriculture has been made Archbishop of Canterbury?!!

DOTTY   Don't shout at *me* . . . I suppose if you think of him as a sort of . . . shepherd, ministering to his flock . . .

GEORGE   But he's an *agnostic*.

DOTTY (*capitulating*)   I absolutely agree with you—*nobody* is going to have any confidence in him. It's like the Chairman of the Coal Board believing in oil.

GEORGE (*shouts*)   No, it is not! (*An exhausted pause.*) You're making it up. You just like to get me going.

DOTTY   Do you find it incredible that a man with a scientific background should be Archbishop of Canterbury?

GEORGE   How the hell do *I* know what I find incredible? Credibility is an expanding field. . . . Sheer disbelief hardly registers on the face before the head is nodding with all the wisdom of instant hindsight. 'Archbishop Clegthorpe? Of course! The inevitable capstone to a career in veterinary medicine!' What happened to the old Archbishop?

DOTTY   He abdicated . . . or resigned or uncoped himself—

GEORGE (*thoughtfully*)   Dis-mantled himself, perhaps.

Dotty turns on the TV: the Moon.

33

Good God! (*At window.*) I can actually *see* Clegthorpe!—marching along, attended by two chaplains in belted raincoats.

DOTTY   Is he wearing a mitre?

GEORGE   Yes. He's blessing people to right and left. He must be drunk.

He stares out of the window, Dotty stares at the TV.

DOTTY   Poor moon man, falling home like Lucifer. (*She turns off the TV: Screen goes white.*) . . . Of course, to somebody *on* it, the moon is always full, so the local idea of a sane action may well differ from ours. (*Pause; stonily.*) When they first landed, it was as though I'd seen a unicorn on the television news. . . . It was very interesting, of course. But it certainly spoiled unicorns. (*Pause.*) I tried to explain it to the analyst when everybody in sight was asking me what was the matter 'What's the matter, darling?' . . . 'What *happened*, baby?' What could I say? I came over funny at work so I went home early. It must happen often enough to a working girl. And why must the damned show go on anyway? So it stopped right then and there, and in a way my retirement was the greatest triumph of my career. Because nobody left.

GEORGE (*to himself*)   Sam Clegthorpe!

DOTTY   For nearly an hour they all sat out front, staring at that stupid spangled moon, and they weren't waiting for their money's worth, they were waiting for *news. Is she all right?* . . . Oh yes, not bad for a bored housewife, eh?—not at all bad for a one-time student amateur bored with keeping house for her professor. And they're still waiting!—my retirement is now almost as long as my career, but they're waiting for me to come back out, and finish my song. And writing me love letters in the mean time. That's right, *not* so bloody bad for a second–class honours with a half-good voice and a certain variety of shakes. It's no good, though. They thought it was overwork or alcohol, but it was just those little grey men in goldfish bowls, clumping about in their lead boots on the television news; it was very interesting,

34

but it certainly spoiled that Juney old moon; and much else besides. . . . The analyst went barking up the wrong tree, of course; I should never have mentioned unicorns to a Freudian.

George turns back from the view.

GEORGE (*serenely*) Archbishop Clegthorpe! That must be the high point of scientism; from here on the Darwinian revolution declines to its own origins. Man has gone ape and God is in the ascendant, and it will end as it began, with him gazing speculatively down on the unpeopled earth as the moon rises over the smoking landscape of vulcanite cliffs and lakes of clinker—not another Herculaneum, but the ash itself.

DOTTY Do you think it is . . . *significant* that it's impossible to imagine anyone building a church on the moon?

GEORGE If God exists, he certainly existed before religion. He is a philosopher's God, logically inferred from self-evident premises. That he should have been taken up by a glorified supporters' club is only a matter of psychological interest.

DOTTY Archie says the Church is a monument to irrationality.

GEORGE If Archie ever chose to relinquish his position as an eminent Vice-Chancellor he would make an excellent buffoon; but since he manages to combine both roles without strain, I don't suppose he ever will. (*He turns and shouts at her with surprising anger.*)

The National Gallery is a monument to irrationality! Every concert hall is a monument to irrationality!—and so is a nicely kept garden, or a lover's favour, or a home for stray dogs! You stupid woman, if rationality were the criterion for things being allowed to exist, the world would be one gigantic field of soya beans!

He picks up his tortoise and balances it lovingly on the palm of his hand, at the level of his mouth.

(*Apologetically.*) Wouldn't it, Pat?

The irrational, the emotional, the whimsical . . . these are the stamp of humanity which makes reason a civilizing force. In a wholly rational society the moralist will be a variety of crank, haranguing the bus queue with the demented certitude of one blessed with privileged information—'Good and evil are metaphysical absolutes!' What did I come in for? (*Looking round.*)

DOTTY All this talk about beans reminds me . . . I left something for Mrs. Doings to put in the oven—Could you———?

GEORGE No, I couldn't. You know where the kitchen is———

DOTTY Where?

GEORGE —and your aristocratic pretence that you know nothing of such things is all very amusing when I'm less busy, but—where's Mrs Thingummy?

DOTTY It's a national holiday. I expect she's down there somewhere, waving a little yellow flag.

GEORGE Oh yes—*she* would be in on it. In fact I can't think of anyone more susceptible to the Rad-Lib philosophy: 'No problem is insoluble given a big enough plastic bag.' (*He's leaving.*)

DOTTY You don't happen to *have* a large plastic bag, do you?

GEORGE Can you remember what I came in for?

DOTTY *Please don't leave me!* I don't want to be left, to cope . . .

GEORGE Dotty, I'm sorry, I must. . . . I'm sorry if it's one of your bad days, but things will get better.

DOTTY There's no question of things getting better.
    Things are one way or they are another way; 'better' is how we see them, Archie says, and I don't personally, very much; though sometimes he makes them seem not so bad after all—no, that's wrong, too: he knows not 'seems'. Things do not *seem*, on the one hand, they *are*; and on the other hand, bad is not what they can *be*. They can be green, or square, or Japanese, loud,

fatal, waterproof or vanilla-flavoured; and the same for actions, which can be *disapproved of*, or comical, unexpected, saddening or good television, variously, depending on who frowns, laughs, jumps, weeps or wouldn't have missed it for the world. Things and actions, you understand, can have any number of real and verifiable properties. But good and bad, better and worse, these are not real properties of things, they are just expressions of our feelings about them.

GEORGE   Archie says.

DOTTY (*pause*)   Unfortunately, I don't feel so good today. If you like, I won't see him. It'll be just you and me under that old-fashioned, silvery harvest moon, occasionally blue, jumped over by cows and coupleted by Junes, invariably shining on the one I love; well-known in Carolina, much loved in Allegheny, familiar in Vermont; (*the screw turning in her*) Keats's bloody moon!—for what has made the sage or poet write but the fair paradise of nature's light—And *Milton's* bloody moon! rising in clouded majesty, at length apparent queen, unveiled her peerless light and o'er the dark her silver mantle threw—And Shelley's sodding maiden, with white fire laden, whom mortals call the——(*weeping*) *Oh yes, things were in place then!*

> *She weeps on George's uncomprehending heart. He strokes her hair. She speaks into his chest.*

Oh, Georgie. . . .

> *He strokes her hair. He doesn't really know what to do. So he plays with her hair for what seems a long time, lifting up her hair, running it through his fingers, looking at it, separating strands of hair. His mind grapples with hair, and then drifts, and stops.*

GEORGE   Have you seen Thumper?

> *He is immediately ashamed of himself. But he has killed it. They separate, Dotty straightens up. George walks to the door, taking his tortoise.*

Did Bertrand Russell ever . . . mention me, after that?

DOTTY (*pause*)   Yes, he did, as a matter of fact. He asked whether you hunted.

There is nothing to do but go, so he goes. Into the Study. He has closed the Bedroom door. The Jumper hangs on the door.

Dotty regards the corpse without expression.

During the next scene in the Study, the light remains in the Bedroom, Dotty, during the scene, lifts the corpse off its hook and sits it in an upstage chair.

George enters the Study. His face is still foamed.

The Secretary has been typing out his dictation.

She hands him the sheets.

The merest trace of interest in the fact that he has shaving foam on his face.

GEORGE   I take it then that we are all agreed that God exists, cries of, 'Oh!', I mean a First Cause, cries of, 'Oh, Oh!', you have not been giving me your proper attention, I will attempt a resume, uproar, cries of 'Resign'—Firstly, is God? Secondly that every series has a first term is a condition that makes God a logical necessity. Thirdly, every series does, the notion of infinity without beginning being rejected *a priori*, thank you. (*Snatches page off desk.*) Fifthly, mathematics is not simply the technique of counting— (*Breaks off. Takes new sheet of paper.*)
   To which end I have brought with me a specially trained tortoise——
   (*Breaks off again.*) Pat!?

He heads back towards the Bedroom where Dotty has just dumped the Jumper into the chair. The chair is upstage facing the audience. Dotty is standing up against the chair with her back to the audience. The tortoise has been left downstage right, so George is going to cross the Bedroom behind Dotty's back. The Jumper's yellow trousers are ill concealed by Dotty's body. George enters.

As George opens the door, Dotty calmly lets her robe slip down her back until it hangs like a drape below her buttocks, her arms, still in the sleeves, held out to the sides; thus concealing the Jumper from view. Thus, she is naked from the thighs up, back view. George glances casually at her as he crosses the room.

GEORGE   *Bottom?*

Dotty lifts the robe to cover her bottom.

Back. . . . Somebody's back . . . ?

He picks up the tortoise, Dotty turns to look at him coquettishly over her shoulder. He is recrossing the room towards the door.

Lulu's back!—in town——Very good! (*He leaves, closing the door, and re-enters the Study. Dotty pulls her robe on again.*)

The Bedroom fades out.

In the Study, he picks up the bow and an arrow.

GEORGE (*to himself*)   The Vice-Chancellor?

The doorbell rings. He hesitates.

He's early. (*Looks at his watch.*) Good God, it's unprofessional conduct. He's only just *left*.

He marches to the door, brandishing his bow and arrow, and, putting his mouth to the tortoise's ear, or thereabouts, confides in it.

Now might I do it, Pat. (*He opens the Front Door. It is* INSPECTOR BONES. *He carries a bunch of flowers. The door is opened to him by a man holding a bow and arrow in one hand and a tortoise in the other, his face covered in shaving foam, Bones recoils from the spectacle, and George is somewhat taken aback too. A rapid exchange follows. . . .*) Yes?

BONES   Ah!——Bones!

GEORGE   What?

BONES   As in rags-and.

GEORGE Rags and bones???

BONES Yes—no. Bones' the name, as in dem bones, dem bones. . . . (*Pause.*) . . . dem dry bones. That's a tortoise is it?

GEORGE I'm sorry, I was expecting a psychiatrist.

BONES No really?

Bones is himself again, master of any situation. He advances past George on the last line.

GEORGE I'm really rather busy.

Bones is now past him. Bones looks at George with unconcealed interest.

BONES What is it that you do?

GEORGE I'm a professor of moral philosophy.

BONES (*wagging a finger*) I'm very glad you said that, son.

Bones continues his inspection of the Hall.

GEORGE Perhaps I can help you.

BONES In my inquiries, you mean, or just generally? Think carefully before you answer—if it gets about that you're helping me in my *inquiries*, bang goes your credit at the off-licence for a start. Inspector Bones, C.I.D.—tell Miss Moore I'm here, there's a good lad.

GEORGE (*rather coldly*) It's *Mrs.* Moore, actually.

BONES Moore is her married name?

GEORGE Yes, Moore is *my* name.

BONES (*shrewdly*) You are the husband.

GEORGE Yes.

BONES Professor . . . Moore.

GEORGE Yes. . . . (*Lightening.*) Yes, I'm something of a logician *myself.*

BONES Really? Sawing ladies in half, that sort of thing?

GEORGE Logician.

(*Bones is casing the Hall expertly, just with his eyes.*) Would you like me to take your flowers, Inspector?

BONES I was hoping to see Miss Moore personally.

GEORGE Well, it's awfully nice of you to come round. . . .

BONES Not at all. If I'm going to arrest her, I can hardly do it by Interflora.

GEORGE Arrest her?

BONES Do not be misled by appearances, Charlie. Miss Moore is a great favourite in the Force and I have knocked down many a man who has defaced her photograph in the station canteen— *but*, the law is implacable, it makes no distinction between rich and poor, famous and anonymous, innocent and——I mean, Jack, if the telephone call which set in motion this inquiry was the whim of a lunatic, as I myself suspect, then I will simply take the opportunity of presenting this token tribute to a fine actress, a great singer and a true lady—after which, I will take my leave, perhaps with her autograph on the cover of this much played much loved gramophone record—(*from a capacious inside-pocket of his raincoat*)—and, who knows? the lingering touch of a kiss brushed against an admirer's cheek . . . (*Reverie. . . .*)

BUT!—if it so happens that there is any truth in the allegations concerning events in this luxury penthouse yesterday night, then there are going to be some bruised petals underfoot as the full majesty of the law comes down on her like a ton of bricks, you take my meaning, Ferdinand? (*Entering the Study.*) Is this the scene of your morals? (*The Secretary stares at him.*)

(*Unnecessarily.*) Don't move.

Bones acts as if he owns the place, picking things up and putting them down; glancing over the typewritten sheets on George's desk.

GEORGE This is my secretary—she and I were just——

41

He catches sight of himself on the fourth-wall mirror (the effect is of a double-take at the audience). He puts down the tortoise and the archery kit, and wipes his face hastily.

Oh—I should explain——

BONES   I prefer to use my imagination. When will your wife be back?

GEORGE   She's in bed—indisposed—waiting for the doctor.

BONES   Lockjaw?

GEORGE   No.

BONES   Then we can have a chat. Is God what?

He is reading the first page of the typescript.

GEORGE   What?——Oh—it's a paper I am presenting to the symposium tonight at the university. I am one of two main speakers on the subject, 'Man—good, bad or indifferent?' The subject is in fact the same every year but there is enough disagreement about its meaning to ensure a regular change of topic. It is the first time I have been asked to speak, you know . . . I had hoped to set British moral philosophy back forty years, which is roughly when it went off the rails, but unfortunately, though my convictions are intact and my ideas coherent, I can't seem to find the words . . .

BONES   Well, 'Are God?' is wrong for a start.

GEORGE   Or rather, the words betray the thoughts they are supposed to express. Even the most generalized truth begins to look like special pleading as soon as you trap it in language. It would be a great opportunity if only I could seize it . . . I mean, it's really the event of the year. (*Pause.*) In the world of moral philosophy, that is.

BONES (*putting down the script*)   It's not a world I move in very much.

42

GEORGE   No.

BONES   Show business is my main interest, closely followed by crime detection. If this is the largest room in the flat I don't think I'll be troubling you long.

GEORGE   Oh. Well . . . the bedroom is about the same size, but of course there's the main living room. . . .

BONES   Living room? Big room?

GEORGE   It is big, yes, it was the ballroom before the place was converted into flats.

BONES   High ceiling?

GEORGE   Yes.

BONES   Ah. Take a troupe of acrobats, would it?

GEORGE (*pause*)   Yes. I'm afraid so.

BONES   Getting my drift, Sidney? Let's have a look.

Bones walks out of the Study. After a moment of nonplussed hesitance, George follows quickly, catching up outside the Study door, which he closes behind him.

GEORGE   Inspector!—I think I can help you in your inquiries. I'm your man. I am the mystery telephone caller.

BONES (*pause*)   You laid information against your wife, sir?

GEORGE   Yes. Well, it was really against myself more than my wife.

BONES   Anonymously. Against yourself?

GEORGE   Yes.

BONES   You have a funny way of going about things. Are you trying to prepare the ground for a plea of insanity?

GEORGE   I don't understand you. I didn't give my name because I could hardly register a complaint about the noise issuing from my own flat. So I pretended to be a neighbour who couldn't sleep.

BONES   Your phone call was about the noise?

GEORGE   Yes.

BONES   You didn't mention—an acrobat?

GEORGE   Did I?

BONES   Or a naked woman swinging from the chandeliers?

GEORGE   Oh yes! I'm ashamed to say I did. I said I saw her from the window opposite. I thought a suggestion of immorality might get the police round more quickly than mere exuberance. Not a word of truth in it, of course. I mean about me being at a window opposite. And I withdraw the complaint anyway; the young woman is of excellent character and notably self-composed as a rule. It was a side of her I'd never seen before. High spirits, no doubt. Incidentally, I don't know who answers the phone at your place but he told me to draw my curtains and remember that I was young once; not what one expects.

BONES (*he produces a notebook*)   Who was at this party . . . ?

GEORGE   Oh . . . academics, writers, doctors, philosophers, actors, musicians, party-workers, acrobats; and of course the Vice-Chancellor who is a bit of everything.

BONES   A mixed bunch.

GEORGE   Not really. I mean, they're all local Rad-Lib celebrities. It was a victory party.

BONES   You were not celebrating it yourself?

GEORGE   No, I'm not interested in politics. I was trying to write my paper. Apart from bunking down on the couch for a couple of hours at dawn, I've been hard at it. Oh, I popped in once or twice, mainly to tell them to keep the music down. My paper was not coming well and I anticipated a strongly argued riposte from Professor McFee, who obviously thought he had the matter well in hand since he was one of the people actually making all the noise.

BONES   Professor McFee?

GEORGE   Professor of Logic, and my chief adversary at the symposium. A very good man in his way, though perhaps I should describe him as generally approved of—he doesn't, of course, believe in good and bad as such.

BONES   Really? How do you mean?

GEORGE   He thinks good and bad aren't actually *good* and *bad* in any absolute or metaphysical sense, he believes them to be categories of our own making, social and psychological conventions which we have evolved in order to make living in groups a practical possibility, in much the same way as we have evolved the rules of tennis without which Wimbledon Fortnight would be a complete shambles, do you see? For example, McFee would hold that when we speak of, say, telling the truth as being 'good', and, er, casual murder as being 'bad', you don't really want to go into all this, do you?

BONES (*his pencil poised, his eyes wide*)   I am enthralled.

GEORGE   Oh. Well, in simple terms he believes that on the whole people should tell the truth all right, and keep their promises, and so on—but on the sole grounds that if everybody went around telling lies and breaking their word as a matter of course, normal life would be impossible. Of course, he is defining normality in terms of the truth being told and promises being kept, etcetera, so the definition is circular and not worth very much, but the point is it allows him to conclude that telling lies is not *sinful* but simply anti-social.

BONES   And murder?

GEORGE   And murder, too, yes.

BONES   He thinks there's nothing *wrong* with killing people?

GEORGE   Well, put like that, of course. . . . But *philosophically*, he doesn't think it's actually, inherently wrong in itself, no.

BONES (*amazed*)   What sort of philosophy is that?

GEORGE   Mainstream, I'd call it. Orthodox mainstream.

Bones scratches his head, George gazes at him innocently.

BONES   How would you describe him—this McFee?

GEORGE   Duncan? Well, he's completely mad, of course. They all are. . . . Well, Inspector, I'm sorry to have wasted your time, but I don't think there's any need to trouble you further. An Englishman's home is his castle, eh?

He opens the Front Door, Bones ignores it.

BONES (*with irony*)   In these cases, we *do* like to have a look at the scene of the crime——

GEORGE   Oh, really? What for?

BONES   It's traditional. . . . Where can I find a vase?

GEORGE   A vase? In the kitchen.

BONES   About mad McFee—has he got a gun?

GEORGE   I don't know. I believe he has a fishing-rod——Oh *no*, you don't understand. He wouldn't *kill* anyone. He's against it. He thinks it shouldn't be allowed. He would prefer it to be kept to a minimum. Otherwise—shambles. He's no more capable of killing someone than the Archbishop of Canterbury. (*Small pause.*) Not *as* capable.

BONES   Well, if that's the case, I don't see any difference whether he thinks he's obeying the Ten Commandments or the rules of tennis.

GEORGE   The difference is, the rules of tennis can be changed.

Immediately: Procession music.

Procession on Screen.

Light up Bedroom.

Bones exits to Kitchen, George closes the Front Door.

Dotty hears the door.

DOTTY   Archie! . . .

Dotty has been watching the TV Screen. The Jumper is hidden.

George goes to the Bedroom door, and opens it.

GEORGE (*from the doorway*)   It's not Archie, it's the police.

Dotty turns off the TV. The Screen goes white.

DOTTY   What?

GEORGE   Inspector Bones. It's about last night. Malicious complaints. Allegations.

DOTTY   What sort of allegations?

GEORGE (*embarrassed, playing it down*)   Anonymous phone call, apparently. Tell you later.

He tries to leave, the first of several false exits by him. Dotty is numb.

DOTTY   Did he mention an acrobat?

GEORGE   Yes. Don't worry, I'll smooth him over.

DOTTY   Smooth him over?

GEORGE   He's gone to inspect the scene of the crime. What an absurd fuss.

DOTTY   George . . . you knew about it?

George mistakes her gratitude for suspicion.

GEORGE   Look, I'm perfectly willing to take the blame.

DOTTY Oh, George . . . George . . . will you?

She kisses him.

GEORGE If he's going to be bloody-minded, I'll shoot him in here.

DOTTY *Georgie!*

GEORGE You can try your charms on him. He's dead keen to meet you. (*False exit.*) He seems quite interested in philosophy.

DOTTY Oh?

GEORGE Yes. I think I can get through to him. Get him to see that one can easily get things out of proportion.

DOTTY (*enthusiastically*) That's just what Archie said about it.

GEORGE (*nods, false exit*) Said about what?

DOTTY Well, about poor Duncan McFee.

GEORGE What about Duncan McFee?

DOTTY There's no need to get it out of proportion. It's a great pity, but it's not as though the alternative were immortality.

GEORGE (*nods; stops nodding*) Sorry?

BONES (*offstage*) Hello! (*Enters from Kitchen.*)

Dotty pushes George out of the Bedroom and closes the door. The Bedroom BLACKS OUT. *George turns to meet Bones who has appeared and is coming upstage, his flowers now in a metal vase.*

BONES Tell me something——Who *are* these acrobats?

GEORGE Logical positivists, mainly, with a linguistic analyst or two, a couple of Benthamite Utilitarians . . . lapsed Kantians and empiricists generally . . . and of course the usual Behaviourists . . . a mixture of the more philosophical members of the university gymnastics team and the more gymnastic members of the

48

Philosophy School. The close association between gymnastics and philosophy is I believe unique to this university and owes itself to the Vice-Chancellor, who is of course a first-rate gymnast, though an indifferent philosopher.

Bones stares at him and then walks into the Study and sits down like a man who needs to sit down. George follows him.

A curious combination of interests, but of course in ancient classical Greece——

BONES   We are not *in* ancient bloody classical Greece.

GEORGE   I absolutely agree with you. In fact, I will have nothing to do with it. And in spite of the Vice-Chancellor's insistence that I can jump better than I think, I have always maintained the opposite to be the case. . . . In the circumstances I was lucky to get the Chair of Moral Philosophy. (*His tone suggests, rightly, that this is not much of a prize.*) Only the Chair of Divinity lies further below the salt, and *that's* been vacant for six months since the last occupant accepted a position as curate in a West Midland diocese.

BONES   Then why didn't you . . . jump along with the rest?

GEORGE   I belong to a school which regards all sudden movements as ill-bred. On the other hand, McFee, who sees professorship as a licence for eccentricity, and whose chief delusion is that Edinburgh is the Athens of the North, very soon learned to jump a great deal better than he ever thought, and was rewarded with the Chair of Logic.

BONES   Are you telling me that the Professor of Logic is a part-time acrobat?

GEORGE   Yes. More of a gymnast, really—the acrobatics are just the social side.

BONES   I find this very hard to believe.

GEORGE   Oh, really? Why's that?

BONES (*rising*)   I don't like it, Clarence! The way I had it, some raving nutter phones up the station with a lot of bizarre allegations starting off with a female person swinging naked from the chandeliers at Dorothy Moore's Mayfair residence and ending up with a professor picked off while doing handsprings for the cabaret, and as far as I'm concerned it's got fruit-cake written all over it; so I tell my Sergeant to have a cup of tea and off I go thinking to myself, at last a chance to pay my respects in person, and blow me if it doesn't start to look straight up as soon as I put one foot in the door——Don't go, will you?

He has moved to the door, with his vase of flowers, and leaves, closing the Study door behind him. In front of the Bedroom door, he briefly smooths his hair, brushes his lapels with his hands, brings out the gramophone record (which has a picture of Dotty on it), and knocks on the Bedroom door, a mere tap, and enters the Bedroom.

The light is romantic: pink curtains have been drawn across the french window, and there is a rosy hue to the lighting.

Dotty, gowned, coiffed, stunning, rises to face the Inspector. Music is heard . . . romantic Mozartian trumpets, triumphant.

Dotty and Bones face each other, frozen like lovers in a dream.

Bones raises his head slightly, and the trumpets are succeeded by a loud animal bray, a mating call, Dotty, her arms out towards him, breathes, 'Inspector . . .' like a verbal caress. From Bones's lifeless fingers, the vase drops. There is a noise such as would have been made had he dropped it down a long flight of stone stairs.

Bones is dumbstruck.

Dotty lets go a long slow smile: 'Inspector. . . .'

From behind the closed curtains, the stiff dead Jumper falls into the room like a too-hastily-leaned plank.

Quick fade to BLACKOUT, *in Bedroom only.*

None of the sounds have been imaginary: they have come from George's coincidental tape-recorder, which he now switches off and rewinds slightly, George picks up his manuscript, snaps his fingers at the Secretary, and starts off.

GEORGE Professor McFee's introductory paper, which it is my privilege to dispute, has I think been distributed to all of you. In an impressive display of gymnastics, ho ho, thank you, Professor McFee bends over backwards to demonstrate that moral judgements belong to the same class as aesthetic judgements; that the phrases 'good man' and 'good music' are prejudiced in exactly the same way; in short, that goodness, whether in men or in music, depends on your point of view. By discrediting the idea of beauty as an aesthetic absolute, he hopes to discredit by association the idea of goodness as a moral absolute and as a first step he directs us to listen to different kinds of music. (*He reaches for the tape-recorder.*) Professor McFee refers us in particular to the idea of beauty as conceived by Mozart on the one hand, and here I am glad to be able to assist him . . . (*Plays the Mozart again, very brief.*) . . . and, on the other hand, as conceived by a group of musicians playing at a wedding feast in a part of Equatorial Africa visited only by the makers of television documentaries, one of which the Professor happened to see on a rare occasion when he wasn't out and about jumping through the Vice-Chancellor's hoop, I can't say that, one of which he happened to see. He invites us to agree with him that beauty is a diverse notion and not a universal one. Personally, I would have agreed to this without demur, but the Professor, whose reading is as wide as his jumping is high . . .

The Secretary raises her head.

. . . all right, all right, the Professor bolsters up his argument with various literary references including a telling extract from *Tarzan of the Apes* in which the boy Tarzan on seeing his face for the first time reflected in a jungle pool, bewails his human ugliness as compared to the beauty of the apes among whom he had grown up. I won't dwell on Professor McFee's inability to distinguish between fact and fiction, but as regards the musical references it might be worth pointing out that the sounds made by Mozart and the Africans might have certain things in common which are not shared by the sound of, say, a bucket of coal being emptied on to a tin roof. Indeed, I have brought with me tonight two further trumpet recordings, starting off with the trumpeting of an elephant . . . (*He plays the braying sound heard before.*) . . . and I invite Professor McFee to admit that the difference between that and his beloved Mozart may owe more to some mysterious property of the music than to his classically trained ear. Anticipating his reply that the latter sound is more beautiful to an elephant, I riposte with . . . (*He plays the remaining sound, as heard before.*) . . . which is the sound made by a trumpet falling down a flight of stone stairs. However, it is not my present concern to dispute Professor McFee's view on aesthetics but only to make clear what those views must lead him to, and they lead him to the conclusion that if the three sets of noises which we might label 'Mozart', 'elephant' and 'stairs', were playing in an empty room where no one could hear them, then it could not be said that within the room any one set of noises was in any way superior to either of the other two. Which may, of course, be the case, but Professor McFee does not stay to consider such a *reductio ad absurdum*, for he has bigger fish to fry, and so he goes on to show, likewise but at even greater length, that the word 'good' has also meant different things to different people at different times, an exercise which combines simplicity with futility in a measure he does not apparently suspect, for on the one hand it is not a statement which anyone would dispute, and on the other, nothing useful can be inferred from it. It is not in fact a statement about value at all; it is a statement about language and how it is used in a particular society. Nevertheless, up this deeply rutted garden path, Professor McFee leads us, pointing out items of interest along the way . . . the tribe which kills its sickly infants, the tribe which eats its aged parents; and so on, without pausing to wonder whether the conditions of group survival or the notion of filial homage might be one thing among the nomads of the Atlas Mountains or in a Brazilian rain forest, and quite another in the Home Counties. Certainly a tribe which believes it confers honour on its elders by eating them is going to be viewed askance by another which prefers to buy them a little bungalow somewhere, and Professor McFee should not be surprised that the notion of honour should manifest itself so differently in peoples so far removed in clime and in culture. What is surely more surprising is that notions such as honour should manifest themselves at all. For what *is* honour? What are pride, shame, fellow-feeling, generosity and love? If they are instincts, what are instincts? The prevailing temper of modern philosophy is to treat the instinct as a sort of terminus for any train of thought that seeks to trace our impulses to their origins. But what can be said to be the impulse of a genuinely altruistic act? Hobbes might have answered self-esteem, but what is the attraction or the point in thinking better of oneself? What is *better*? A savage who elects to honour his father by eating him as opposed to disposing of the body in some—to him—ignominious way, for example by burying it in a teak box, is making an ethical choice in that he believes himself to be acting as a good savage ought to act. Whence comes this sense of some actions being better than others?—not more useful, or more convenient, or more popular, but simply pointlessly *better*? What, in short, is so good about *good*? Professor McFee succeeds only in showing us that in different situations different actions will be deemed, rightly or wrongly, to be conducive to that good which is independent of time and place and which is knowable but not nameable. It is not nameable because it is not another way or referring to this or that quality which we have decided is virtuous. It is not courage, and it is not honesty or loyalty or kindness. The irreducible fact of goodness is not implicit in one kind of action any more than in its opposite, but in the existence of a relationship between the two. It is the sense of comparisons being in order.

Music! Lights! Dorothy Moore—in person!

. . . In fact, a track from Dotty's record, playing in the Bedroom, and Dotty swinging and miming to it, as Bones leaves the Bedroom, the

*opening of the door triggering off the scene, George also goes into the
Hall, where he meets Bones.*

We can't hear what they say because the music is loud.

*George takes Bones downstage to the Kitchen exit, and goes off with
him. Dotty continues to sway and mime: the song is 'Sentimental
Journey'.*

The dead Jumper is where he fell.

The Secretary moves to the typewriter.

*The Front Door opens and Archie enters, and stops just inside the door,
almost closing it behind him. He stands listening—an impressive figure,
exquisitely dressed orchid in buttonhole, cigarette in long black holder,
and everything which those details suggest. He carefully opens the door of
the Study. The Secretary looks up. She nods at him, but it is impossible
to draw any conclusions from that.*

*Archie withdraws, closing the door. He comes downstage and looks along
the corridor into the Kitchen wing. He returns to the Front Door and
opens it wide.*

*Seven Jumpers in yellow tracksuits enter smoothly, four of them carry a
machine of ambiguous purpose: it might be a television camera. They
also carry a couple of lights on tall stands, suitable for filming (these items
may be all in one box). Six enter the Bedroom, Archie opening the door
for them.*

One Jumper goes downstage to watch the Kitchen exit.

*In the Bedroom, Dotty is surprised but pleased by the entry of Archie
and the Jumpers. They put down the 'camera' and the lights. They have
come to remove the body.*

*The song dominates the whole scene. Nothing else can be heard, and
its beat infects the business of removing the body, for Dotty continues to
sway and snap her fingers as she moves about welcoming the troops, and
the Jumpers lightly respond, so that the effect is a little simple improvised
choreography between the Jumpers and Dotty.*

Archie moves downstage, facing front, and like a magician about to demonstrate a trick, takes from his pocket a small square of material like a handkerchief, which he unfolds and unfolds and unfolds until it is a large plastic bag, six feet tall, which he gives to two Jumpers. These two hold the mouth of the bag open at the door; as the climax of the 'dance' the four Jumpers throw the body into the bag: bag closes, Bedroom door closes, Jumpers moving smoothly, Front Door closes, and on the last beat of the song, only Archie and Dotty are left onstage.

BLACKOUT

END OF ACT ONE

ACT TWO

The Bedroom is BLACKED OUT, *but music still comes from it—presumably the next track on the album.* Only a minute or two have passed.*

Bones appears from the Kitchen entrance. He is pushing a well-laden dinner-trolley in front of him. It has on it a covered casserole dish, a bottle of wine in an ice bucket, two glasses, two plates, two of everything . . . dinner for two in fact, and very elegant.

He is followed by George holding a couple of lettuce leaves and a carrot, which he nibbles absently.

GEORGE   What do you mean, 'What does he look like?' He looks like a rabbit with long legs.

But Bones has stopped, listening to Dotty's voice, rather as a man might pause in St. Peter's on hearing choristers. . . .

BONES   That was it. . . . That was the one she was singing. . . .

I remember how her voice faltered, I saw the tears spring into her eyes, the sobs shaking her breast . . . and that awful laughing scream as they brought the curtain down on the first lady of the musical stage—never to rise again! Oh yes, there are many stars in the West End night, but there's only ever been one Dorothy Moore. . . .

GEORGE   Yes, I must say I envy her that. There have not been so many philosophers, but *two* of them have been George Moore, and it tends to dissipate the impact of one's name. But for that, I think

---

* The song "Forget Yesterday," composed by Marc Wilkinson with lyrics by Tom Stoppard, is printed on page 94.

57

my book *Conceptual Problems of Knowledge and Mind* would have caused quite a stir.

BONES   Any chance of a come-back, sir?

GEORGE   Well, I'm still hoping to find a publisher for it. I have also made a collection of my essays under the title, *Language, Truth and God*. An American publisher has expressed an interest but he wants to edit it himself and change the title to *You Better Believe It*. . . . I suppose it would be no worse than benefitting from my wife's gramophone records.

BONES   A consummate artist, sir. I felt it deeply when she retired.

GEORGE   Unfortunately she retired from consummation about the same time as she retired from artistry.

BONES   It was a personal loss, really.

GEORGE   Quite. She just went off it. I don't know why.

BONES (*coming round to him at last*)   You don't have to explain to me, sir. You can't keep much from her hard-core fans. Actually, I had a brother who had a nervous breakdown.
   It's a terrible thing. It's the pressure, you know. The appalling pressure of being a star.

GEORGE   Was your brother a star?

BONES   No, he was an osteopath. Bones the Bones, they called him. Every patient had to make a little joke. It drove him mad, finally.

They have been approaching the Bedroom door, but Bones suddenly abandons the trolley and takes George downstage.

(*Earnestly.*) You see, Dorothy is a delicate creature, like a lustrous-eyed little bird you could hold in your hand, feeling its little brittle bones through its velvety skin—vulnerable, you understand; highly strung. No wonder she broke under the strain. And you don't get over it, just like that. It can go on for years, the effect, afterwards—

58

building up again, underneath, until, one day—*Snap!*—do something violent perhaps, quite out of character, you know what I mean? It would be like a blackout. She wouldn't know what she was doing. (*He grips George's elbow.*) And I should think that any competent or, better still, eminent psychiatric expert witness would be prepared to say so. Of course, he wouldn't be cheap, but it can be done, do you follow me?

GEORGE (*puzzled*)   I'm not sure that I do.

BONES   Well, your wife says you can explain everything, and you say you are wholly responsible, but——

GEORGE   Are you still going on about that?—for goodness sake, I just lost my temper for a moment, that's all, and took matters into my own hands.

BONES   Because of the noise?

GEORGE   Exactly.

BONES   Don't you think it was a bit extreme?

GEORGE   Yes, yes, I suppose it was a bit.

BONES   Won't wash, Wilfred. I believe you are trying to shield her.

GEORGE   Shield who?

BONES   It's quite understandable. Is there a man who could stand aside when this fair creature is in trouble——

GEORGE   Aren't you getting a little carried away? The point is, surely, that I'm the householder and I must be held responsible for what happens in my house.

BONES   I don't think the burden of being a householder extends to responsibility for any crime committed on the premises.

GEORGE   Crime? You call that a crime?

BONES (*with more heat*)   Well, what would you call it?

GEORGE It was just a bit of *fun*! Where's your sense of humour, man?

BONES (*staggered*) I don't know, you bloody philosophers are all the same, aren't you? A man is dead and you're as cool as you like. Your wife begged me with tears in her eyes to go easy on you, and I don't mind admitting I was deeply moved——

GEORGE Excuse me——

BONES (*angrily*) But you're wasted on her, mate. What on earth made *her* marry *you*, I'll never know, when there are so many better men—decent, strong, protective, understanding, sensitive——

GEORGE Did you say somebody was dead?

BONES Stone dead, in the bedroom.

GEORGE Don't be ridiculous.

BONES The body is lying on the floor!

GEORGE (*going to door*) You have obviously taken leave of your senses.

BONES Don't touch it!—it will have to be examined for fingerprints.

GEORGE If there is a body on the floor, it will have my *footprints* on it.

He opens the Bedroom door. In the Bedroom, no one is in view. The drapes—or screens—are round the bed. The ambiguous machine— the dermatograph—is set up so that it peers with its lens through the drapes. The camera-lights are in position round the bed, shining down over the drapes into the bed. The TV set is connected by a lead to the dermatograph.

George pauses in the doorway.

ARCHIE (*within*) . . . There . . .

DOTTY (*within*) . . . Yes . . .

ARCHIE There . . . there . . .

DOTTY Yes . . .

ARCHIE . . . and there . . .

DOTTY Yes . . . yes.

These sounds are consistent with a proper doctor-patient relationship. If Dotty has a tendency to gasp slightly it is probably because the stethoscope is cold, Archie on the other hand, might be getting rather overheated under the blaze of the dermatograph lights.

ARCHIE (*within*) Excuse me . . .

Archie's coat comes sailing over the drapes. George retreats, closing the door.

GEORGE Well, he's very much alive now.

BONES Sir?

GEORGE My wife's doctor.

BONES Really? On the floor?

GEORGE He's a psychiatrist, notorious for his methods. And for much else. (*On this bitter note, George goes into the Study, Bones, with the trolley, cautiously enters the Bedroom. No one is in view. Bones pauses. One of Archie's shoes comes over the drapes and falls on the floor. Another pause. The second shoe comes over, falling into Bones's hands. The absence of a thump brings Archie's head into view, popping up over the drapes.*)

ARCHIE Ah! Good morning!

Archie moves to come out from the bed. Meanwhile Dotty looks over the top.

DOTTY Lunch! And Bonesy!

Archie picks his coat up and hands it to Bones, and then readies himself to put his arms in the sleeves, as though Bones were a manservant.

ARCHIE (*slipping on his coat*)   Thank you so much. Rather warm in there. The lights, you know.

DOTTY   Isn't he sweet?

ARCHIE   Charming. What happened to Mrs. Whatsername?

DOTTY   No, no, it's Bonesy!

BONES   Inspector Bones, C.I.D.

DOTTY (*disappearing*)   Excuse me!

ARCHIE   Bones . . . ? I had a patient named Bones. I wonder if he was any relation?—an osteopath.

BONES   My brother!

ARCHIE   Remember the case well. Cognomen Syndrome. My advice to him was to take his wife's maiden name of Foot and carry on from there.

BONES   He took your advice but unfortunately he got interested in chiropody. He is now in an asylum near Uxbridge.

ARCHIE   Isn't that interesting? I must write him up. The Cognomen Syndrome is my baby, you know.

BONES   You discovered it?

ARCHIE   I've got it. Jumper's the name—my card.

BONES (*reading off card*)   'Sir Archibald Jumper, M.D., D.Phil., D. Litt., L.D., D.P.M., D.P.T. (*Gym*)'. . . . What's all that?

ARCHIE   I'm a doctor of medicine, philosophy, literature and law, with diplomas in psychological medicine and P.T. including gym.

BONES (*handing back the card*)   I see that you are the Vice-Chancellor of Professor Moore's university.

ARCHIE   Not a bad record, is it? And I can still jump over seven feet.

BONES   High jump?

ARCHIE   Long jump. My main interest, however, is the trampoline.

BONES   Mine is show business generally.

ARCHIE   Really? Well, nowadays, of course, I do more theory than practice, but if trampoline acts appeal to you at all, a vacancy has lately occurred in a little team I run, mainly for our own amusement with a few social engagements thrown in——

BONES   Just a minute, just a minute!—what happened to Professor McFee?

ARCHIE   Exactly. I regret to tell you he is dead.

BONES   I realize he is *dead*——

ARCHIE   Shocking tragedy. I am entirely to blame.

BONES   You, too, sir?

ARCHIE   Yes, Inspector.

BONES   Very chivalrous, sir, but I'm afraid it won't wash.
   (*He addresses the drapes, loudly.*) Miss Moore, is there anything you wish to say at this stage?

DOTTY (*her head appearing*)   Sorry?

BONES   My dear—we are all *sorry*——

   Dotty appears.

ARCHIE   Just a moment! I will not have a patient of mine browbeaten by the police.

BONES (*thoughtfully*)   Patient . . .

ARCHIE   Yes. As you can see I have been taking a dermatographical reading.

BONES (*indicating the dermatograph*)   This? What does it do?

ARCHIE   It reads the skin, electronically; hence dermatograph.

BONES   Why is it connected to the television set?

ARCHIE   We'll get the read-back on the screen. All kinds of disturbances under the skin show up on the surface, if we can learn to read it, and we are learning.

BONES   Disturbances? Mental disturbances?

ARCHIE   Among other things.

BONES (*a new intimacy*)   Sir Jim――

ARCHIE   Archie――

BONES   Sir Archie, might I have a word with you, in private?

ARCHIE   Just what I was about to suggest. (*He opens the Bedroom door.*) Shall we step outside . . . ?

Bones steps into the Hall.

DOTTY   . . . Things don't seem so bad after all. So to speak.

Archie follows Bones into the Hall. Fade out on Bedroom, Archie and Bones move towards Kitchen exit.

BONES   This is just between you and me, Sigmund. I understand your feelings only too well. What decent man could stand aside while that beautiful, frail creature――(*In the Study, George has resumed . . .*)

GEORGE   The study of moral philosophy is an attempt to determine what we mean when we say that something is good and that something else is bad. Not all value judgements, however, are the proper study of the moral philosopher. Language is a finite instrument crudely applied to an infinity of ideas, and one consequence of the failure to take account of this is that modern philosophy has made itself ridiculous by analysing such statements as, 'This is a good bacon sandwich,' or, 'Bedser had a good wicket.' (*The Secretary raises her head at 'Bedser'.*) Bedser!—Good God, B-E-D-S . . .

Fade on Study.

Archie and Bones re-enter.

ARCHIE   Please come to the point, Inspector. The plain facts are that while performing some modest acrobatics for the entertainment of Miss Moore's party-guests, Professor McFee was killed by a bullet fired from the outer darkness. We all saw him shot, but none of us saw who shot him. With the possible exception of McFee's fellow gymnasts, anybody could have fired the shot, and anybody could have had a reason for doing so, including, incidentally, myself.

BONES   And what might *your* motive be, sir?

ARCHIE   Who knows? Perhaps McFee, my faithful protégé, had secretly turned against me, gone off the rails and decided that he was St. Paul to Moore's Messiah.

BONES   Doesn't seem much of a reason.

ARCHIE   It depends. Moore himself is not important—he is our tame believer, pointed out to visitors in much the same spirit as we point out the magnificent stained glass in what is now the gymnasium. But McFee was the guardian and figurehead of philosophical orthodoxy, and if he threatened to start calling on his masters to return to the true path, then I'm afraid it would certainly have been an ice-pick in the back of the skull.

DOTTY (*off*)   Darling!

ARCHIE   And then again, perhaps it was Dorothy. Or someone.

Smiles.

DOTTY (*off*)   Darling!

BONES   My advice to you is, number one, get her lawyer over here——

ARCHIE   That will not be necessary. I am Miss Moore's legal adviser.

BONES   Number two, completely off the record, get her off on expert evidence—nervous strain, appalling pressure, and one day—

snap!—blackout, can't remember a thing. Put her in the box and you're half-way there. The other half is, get something on Mad Jock McFee, and if you don't get a Scottish judge it'll be three years probation and the sympathy of the court.

ARCHIE This is most civil of you, Inspector, but a court appearance would be most embarrassing to my client and patient; and three years' probation is not an insignificant curtailment of a person's liberty.

BONES For God's sake, man, we're talking about a murder charge.

ARCHIE You are. What I had in mind is that McFee, suffering from nervous strain brought on by the appalling pressure of overwork—for which I blame myself entirely—left here last night in a mood of deep depression, and wandered into the park, where he crawled into a large plastic bag and shot himself . . .

   Pause, Bones opens his mouth to speak.

. . . leaving this note . . . (*Archie produces it from his pocket.*) . . . which was found in the bag together with his body by some gymnasts on an early morning keep-fit run. (*Pause. Bones opens his mouth to speak.*) Here is the coroner's certificate.

   Archie produces another note, which Bones takes from him. Bones reads it.

BONES Is this genuine?

ARCHIE (*testily*) Of course it's genuine. I'm a coroner, not a forger.

   Bones hands the certificate back, and almost comes to attention.

BONES Sir Archibald Bouncer——

ARCHIE Jumper.

BONES Sir Archibald Jumper, I must——

ARCHIE Now, I judge from your curiously formal and somewhat dated attitude, that you are deaf to offers of large sums of money for favours rendered.

BONES I didn't hear that.

ARCHIE Exactly. On the other hand, I think you are a man who feels that his worth has not been recognized. Other men have got on—younger men, flashier men . . . Superintendents . . . Commissioners. . . .

BONES There may be something in that.

ARCHIE I dare say your ambitions do not stop with the Police Force, even.

BONES Oh?

ARCHIE Inspector, my patronage is not extensive, but it is select. I can offer prestige, the respect of your peers and almost unlimited credit among the local shopkeepers—in short, the Chair of Divinity is yours for the asking.

BONES The Chair of Divinity?

ARCHIE Not, perhaps, the Chair which is in the eye of the hurricane nowadays, but a professorship will still be regarded as a distinction come the day—early next week, in all probability—when the Police Force will be thinned out to a ceremonial front for the peace-keeping activities of the Army.

BONES I see. Well, until that happens, I should still like to know—if McFee shot himself inside a plastic bag, where is the gun?

ARCHIE (*awed*) Very good thinking indeed! On consideration I can give you the Chair of Logic, but that is my last offer.

BONES This is a British murder enquiry and some degree of justice must be seen to be more or less done.

ARCHIE I must say I find your attitude lacking in flexibility. What makes you so sure that it *was* Miss Moore who shot McFee?

BONES   I have a nose for these things.

ARCHIE   With the best will in the world I can't give the Chair of Logic to a man who relies on nasal intuition.

DOTTY (*off*)   Help!

Bones reacts, Archie restrains him.

ARCHIE   It's all right—just exhibitionism: what we psychiatrists call 'a cry for help'.

BONES   But it *was* a cry for help.

ARCHIE   Perhaps I'm not making myself clear. *All* exhibitionism is a cry for help, but a cry for help *as such* is only exhibitionism.

DOTTY (*off*)   MURDER!

Bones rushes to the Bedroom, which remains dark, Archie looks at his watch and leaves towards the Kitchen. In the Study George resumes.

GEORGE   . . . whereas a spell with the heavy roller would improve it from Bradman's point of view and worsen it from Bedser's . . .

Likewise, to say that this is a good bacon sandwich is only to say that by the criteria applied by like-minded lovers of bacon sandwiches, this one is worthy of approbation. The word good is reducible to other properties such as crisp, lean and unadulterated by tomato sauce. You will have seen at once that to a man who likes his bacon sandwiches underdone, fatty and smothered in ketchup, this would be a rather *poor* bacon sandwich. By subjecting any given example to similar analysis, the modern school, in which this university has played so lamentable a part, has satisfied itself that all statements implying goodness or badness, whether in conduct or in bacon sandwiches, are not statements of *fact* but merely expressions of feeling, taste or vested interest.

But when we say that the Good Samaritan acted well, we are surely expressing more than a circular prejudice about behaviour. We mean he acted kindly—selflessly—*well*. And what is our approval of kindness based on if not on the intuition that kindness is simply good in itself and cruelty is not. A man who sees that he is about to put his foot down on a beetle in his path, decides to step on it or not to. Why? What process is at work? And what is that quick blind mindless connection suddenly made and lost by the man who didn't see the beetle but only heard the crunch? (*Towards the end of this speech, Archie re-enters and quietly lets himself into the Study.*)

It is ironic that the school which denies the claims of the intuition to know good when it sees it, is itself the product of the pioneer work set out in his *Principia Ethica* by the late G. E. Moore, an intuitionist philosopher whom I respected from afar but who, for reasons which will be found adequate by logical spirits, was never in when I called. Moore did not believe in God, but I do not hold that against him—for of all forms of wishful thinking, humanism demands the greatest sympathy— and at least by insisting that goodness was a fact, and on his right to recognize it when he saw it, Moore avoided the moral limbo devised by his successors, who are in the unhappy position of having to admit that one man's idea of good is no more meaningful than another man's whether he be St. Francis or—Vice Chancellor! (*For he has noticed Archie in the mirror. Archie comes forward.*)

ARCHIE   An inept comparison, if I may say so. I'm very fond of animals. (*He picks up* PAT.) What do you call it?

GEORGE   Pat.

ARCHIE   Pat! . . . what a lovely name.

GEORGE   It's a good name for a tortoise, being sexually ambiguous. I also have a hare called Thumper, somewhere. . . . By the way, I wasn't really comparing *you* with——

ARCHIE   Quite understand. You were going to say Hitler or Stalin or Nero . . . the argument always gets back to some lunatic tyrant, the *reductio ad absurdum* of the new ethics, and the dog-eared trump card of the intuitionists.

GEORGE (*rising to that*) Well, why not? When I push *my* convictions to absurdity, *I* arrive at God—which is at least as embarrassing nowadays. (*Pause.*) All I know is that I think that I know that I know that nothing can be created out of nothing, that my moral conscience is different from the rules of my tribe, and that there is more in me than meets the microscope—and because of *that* I'm lumbered with this incredible, indescribable and definitely shifty *God*, the trump card of atheism.

ARCHIE It's always been a mystery to me why religious faith and atheism should be thought of as opposing attitudes.

GEORGE Always?

ARCHIE It just occurred to me.

GEORGE It occurred to you that belief in God and the conviction that God doesn't exist amount to much the same thing?

ARCHIE It gains from careful phrasing. Religious faith and atheism differ mainly about God; about Man they are in accord: Man is the highest form of life, he has duties he has rights, etcetera, and it is usually better to be kind than cruel. Even if there is some inscrutable divinity behind it all, our condition for good or ill is apparently determined by our choice of actions, and choosing seems to be a genuine human possibility. Indeed, it is surely religious zeal rather than atheism which is historically notorious in the fortunes of mankind.

GEORGE I'm not at all sure that the God of religious observance is the object of my faith. Do you suppose it would be presumptuous to coin a deity?

ARCHIE I don't see the point. If he caught on, you'd kill for him, too. (*Suddenly remembering.*) Ah!—I knew there was something!—McFee's dead.

GEORGE What?!!

ARCHIE Shot himself this morning, in the park, in a plastic bag.

GEORGE My God! Why?

ARCHIE It's hard to say. He was always tidy.

GEORGE But to shoot himself . . .

ARCHIE Oh, he could be very violent, you know . . . In fact we had a furious row last night—perhaps the Inspector had asked you about that . . . ?

GEORGE No . . .

ARCHIE It was a purely trivial matter. He took offence at my description of Edinburgh as the Reykjavik of the South.

George is not listening.

GEORGE . . . Where did he find the despair . . . ? I thought the whole *point* of denying the Absolute was to reduce the scale, instantly, to the inconsequential behaviour of inconsequential animals; that nothing could ever be that important . . .

ARCHIE Including, I suppose, death. . . . It's an interesting view of atheism, as a sort of *crutch* for those who can't bear the reality of God.

GEORGE (*still away*) I wonder if McFee was afraid of death? And if he was, what was it that he would have been afraid of: surely not the chemical change in the material that was his body. I suppose he would have said, as so many do, that it is only the dying he feared, yes, the physical process of giving out. But it's not the dying with me—one knows about pain. It's *death* that I'm afraid of. (*Pause.*)

ARCHIE Incidentally, since his paper has of course been circulated to everyone, it must remain the basis of the symposium.

GEORGE Yes, indeed, I have spent weeks preparing my commentary on it.

ARCHIE We shall begin with a two-minute silence. That will give me a chance to prepare mine.

GEORGE   You will be replying, Vice-Chancellor?

ARCHIE   At such short notice I don't see who else could stand in. I'll relinquish the chair, of course, and we'll get a new chairman, someone of good standing; he won't have to know much philosophy. Just enough for a tribute to Duncan.

GEORGE   Poor Duncan . . . I like to think he'll be there in spirit.

ARCHIE   If only to make sure the materialistic argument is properly represented.

DOTTY (*off*)   Darling!

Both men respond automatically, and both halt and look at each other.

GEORGE / ARCHIE   How is she?

GEORGE   How do I know? You're the doctor.

ARCHIE   That's true.

Archie moves out of the Study, George with him; into the Hall.

I naturally try to get her to open up, but one can't assume she tells me everything, or even that it's the truth.

GEORGE   Well, I don't know what's the matter with her. She's like a cat on hot bricks, and doesn't emerge from her room. All she says is, she's all right in bed.

ARCHIE   Yes, well there's something in that.

GEORGE (*restraining his going; edgily*)   What exactly do you do in there?

ARCHIE   Therapy takes many forms.

GEORGE   I had no idea you were still practising.

ARCHIE   Oh yes . . . a bit of law, a bit of philosophy, a bit of medicine, a bit of gym. . . . A bit of one and then a bit of the other.

GEORGE   You examine her?

ARCHIE   Oh yes, I like to keep my hand in. You must understand, my dear Moore, that when I'm examining Dorothy I'm not a lawyer or a philosopher. Or a gymnast, of course. Oh, I know, my dear fellow—you think that when I'm examining Dorothy I see her eyes as cornflowers, her lips as rubies, her skin as soft and warm as velvet—you think that when I run my hands over her back I am carried away by the delicate contours that flow like a sea-shore from shoulder to heel—oh yes, you think my mind turns to ripe pears as soon as I press——

GEORGE (*viciously*)   No, I don't!

ARCHIE   But to us medical men, the human body is just an imperfect machine. As it is to most of us philosophers. And to us gymnasts, of course.

DOTTY (*off; urgently*)   R apel (*Pause.*) Ru———!

Archie smiles at George, and quickly lets himself into the Bedroom, closing the door behind him.

The Bedroom lights up. The dermatograph and the lights have been put away. The bed is revealed as before, Dotty is sobbing across the bed.

Bones standing by as though paralysed. A wild slow smile spreads over his face as he turns to Archie, the smile of a man pleading, 'It's not what you think.' Archie moves in slowly.

ARCHIE   Tsk tsk . . . Inspector, I am shocked . . . deeply shocked. What a tragic end to an incorruptible career . .

BONES   . . . I never touched her——

ARCHIE   Do not despair. I'm sure we can come to some arrangement. . . .

George has returned to the Study.

GEORGE   How the hell does one know what to believe?

Fade out on Bedroom, to BLACKOUT.

The Secretary has taken down the last sentence.

GEORGE No, no——(*Changes mind.*) Well, all right. (*Dictating.*) How does one know what it is one believes when it's so difficult to know what it is one knows. I don't claim to *know* that God exists, I only claim that he does without my knowing it, and while I claim as much I do not claim to know as much; indeed I cannot know and God knows I cannot. (*Pause.*) And yet I tell you that, now and again, not necessarily in the contemplation of polygons or new-born babes, nor in extremities of pain or joy, but more probably ambushed by some quite trivial moment—say the exchange of signals between two long-distance lorry-drivers in the black sleet of a god-awful night on the old Ai—then, in that dip-flash, dip-flash of headlights in the rain that seems to affirm some common ground that is not animal and not long-distance lorry-driving—then I tell you I *know*—I sound like a joke vicar, new paragraph.

(*The light is fading to a spot on George, sufficiently to put the Hall and Front Door into* BLACKOUT *if they are not black already.*) There is in mathematics a concept known as a limiting curve, that is the curve defined as the limit of a polygon with an infinite number of sides. For example, if I had never seen a circle and didn't know how to draw one, I could nevertheless postulate the existence of circles by thinking of them as regular polygons with numberless edges, so that an old threepennybit would be a bumpy imperfect circle which would approach perfection if I kept doubling the number of its sides at infinity the result would be the circle which I have never seen and do not know how to draw, and which is logically implied by the existence of polygons. And now and again, not necessarily in the contemplation of rainbows or new-born babes, nor in extremities of pain or joy, but more probably in some quite trivial moment, it seems to me that life itself is the mundane figure which argues perfection at its limiting curve. And if I doubt it, the ability to doubt, to question, to *think* seems to be the curve itself. *Cogito ergo deus est.* (*Pause.*) The fact that I cut a ludicrous figure in the academic world is largely due to my aptitude for traducing a complex and logical thesis to a mysticism of staggering banality. McFee never made that mistake, never put himself at risk by finding mystery in the clockwork, never looked for trouble or over his shoulder, and I'm sorry he's gone but what can be his complaint? McFee jumped, and left nothing behind but a vacancy.

There is a delicious unraped laugh from Dotty in the dark.

The Study light comes on again; only the Bedroom is BLACKED *as George strides out of the Study; then the Bedroom is lit.*

Archie and Dotty are sitting at the trolley eating a very civilized lunch.

Bones has gone.

DOTTY   I must say, I do find mashed potatoes and gravy very consoling.

George enters without knocking.

GEORGE   I'm sorry to interrupt your inquiries——

He looks round for the Inspector.

Archie smoothly takes a silver-backed notebook from his pocket, and a silver pencil from another.

ARCHIE   When did you first become aware of these feelings?

DOTTY (*gaily*)   I don't know—I've *always* found mashed potatoes and gravy very consoling.

GEORGE   Where's the Inspector?

ARCHIE   The inquiries have been completed. Did you want him?

GEORGE   Well no. . . . As a matter of fact, I came to ask you . . . Vice-Chancellor, about the Chair of Logic.

George is unsettled by the lunch-party atmosphere. Nothing about Archie or Dotty suggests that there is anything unusual about it. They continue to eat and drink.

ARCHIE   Yes?

GEORGE   You probably have had very little time to think about McFee's successor. . . .

ARCHIE The appointment to the Chair of Logic is of course a matter for the gravest consideration. We've always been a happy team and I shall be looking for someone who will fit in, someone with a bit of bounce.

GEORGE Yes. Well, it just seemed to me that as the senior professor——

ARCHIE The oldest——

GEORGE The longest-serving professor——

ARCHIE Oh yes.

GEORGE Well, Logic has traditionally been considered the senior Chair. . . .

ARCHIE (*pause*) Yes, well, there you are; you have made your request. But I'm not too happy about your Ethics.

GEORGE I'm not seeking any favours——

ARCHIE No, no, I mean Ethics has always been your department—what will happen to Ethics?

GEORGE There's no conflict there. My work on moral philosophy has always been based on logical principles, and it would do no harm at all if the Chair of Logic applied itself occasionally to the activities of the human race.

ARCHIE Yes . . . yes. . . . But you see, the Chair of Logic is considered the leading edge of philosophical inquiry here, and *your* strong point is, how shall I put it, well, many of the students are under the impression that you are the author of *Principia Ethica*.

GEORGE But he's dead.

ARCHIE That is why I take a serious view of the mistake.

GEORGE (*pause*) I see. (*Moves towards door.*) Incidentally, what do you psychiatrists call *this* form of therapy?

ARCHIE   Lunch. I don't wish to make a fetish of denying you chairs, but you will appreciate that I can't ask you to sit down—a psychiatrist is akin to a priest taking confession.

DOTTY   Well, it wasn't *me*.

ARCHIE   Absolute privacy, absolute trust.

DOTTY   *I* didn't do it. I thought *you* did it.

GEORGE   What is she talking about? Where's the Inspector?

DOTTY   He's gone. Dishonour is even. (*Giggles.*)

GEORGE   Without taking his record?

DOTTY   Oh yes, we must send it on. I signed it with a most moving dedication, I thought. I forgot what it was, but it was most moving.

George can't put his finger on it, but something is bothering him. He starts to wander towards the Bathroom.

GEORGE   I'm surprised he just . . . went . . . like that.

George enters the Bathroom.

DOTTY   Oh yes——'To Evelyn Bones, the Sweetheart of the Force!'

GEORGE (*off; horrified*)   My God!
   (*George enters from the Bathroom, white, shaking with rage.*) You murderous *bitch*! . . . You might have put some water in the bath!

He is holding a dead goldfish.

DOTTY   Oh dear . . . I am sorry. I forgot about it.

GEORGE   Poor little Arch——(*Catches himself.*)

Archie raises his head a fraction.

GEORGE   Murdered for a charade!

DOTTY (*angrily*)   Murdered? Don't you dare splash *me* with your sentimental rhetoric! It's a bloody goldfish! Do you think every *sole meunière* comes to you untouched by suffering?

GEORGE   The monk who won't walk in the garden for fear of treading on an ant does not have to be a vegetarian. . . . There is an irrational difference which has a rational value.

DOTTY   Brilliant! You must publish your findings in some suitable place like the *Good Food Guide.*

GEORGE   No doubt your rebuttal would look well in the *Meccano Magazine.*

DOTTY   You bloody humbug!—the last of the metaphysical egocentrics! You're probably still shaking from the four-hundred-year-old news that the sun doesn't go round *you!*

GEORGE   We are *all* still shaking. Copernicus cracked our confidence, and Einstein smashed it: for if one can no longer believe that a twelve-inch ruler is always a foot long, how can one be sure of relatively less certain propositions, such as that God made the Heaven and the Earth. . . .

DOTTY (*dry, drained*)   Well, it's all over now. Not only are we no longer the still centre of God's universe, we're not even uniquely graced by his footprint in man's image. . . . Man is on the Moon, his feet on solid ground, and he has seen us whole, all in one go, *little—local* . . . and all our absolutes, the thou-shalts and the thou-shalt-nots that seemed to be the very condition of our existence, how did *they* look to two moonmen with a single neck to save between them? Like the local customs of another place. When that thought drips through to the bottom, people won't just carry on. There is going to be such . . . breakage, such gnashing of unclean meats, such coveting of neighbours' oxen and knowing of neighbours' wives, such dishonourings of mothers and fathers, and bowings and scrapings to images graven and incarnate, such killing of goldfish and maybe more——(*Looks up, tear-stained.*) Because the truths that have been taken on trust, they've never had edges before, there was no vantage point to stand on and see where they stopped. (*And weeps.*)

ARCHIE (*pause*)   When did you first become aware of these feelings?

DOTTY   Georgie. . . .

But George won't or can't. . . .

GEORGE (*facing away, out front, emotionless*)   Meeting a friend in a corridor, Wittgenstein said: 'Tell me, why do people always say it was *natural* for men to assume that the sun went round the earth rather than that the earth was rotating?' His friend said, 'Well, obviously, because it just *looks* as if the sun is going round the earth.' To which the philosopher replied, 'Well, what would it have looked like if it had looked as if the earth was rotating?'

ARCHIE   I really can't conduct a consultation under these conditions! You might as well join us.

GEORGE (*moving*)   No, thank you.

ARCHIE   Do . . . This, whatever it is, makes a very good casserole.

DOTTY (*dry-eyed revenge*)   It's not casseroled. It's jugged.

George freezes. Pause.

Doorbell.

GEORGE   Dorothy. . . .

DOTTY   Somebody at the door.

It's Crouch, who rings the bell out of formality and lets himself in with his master key, pausing in the door so as not to intrude on anything, announcing himself: 'Crouch!'

GEORGE   Dorothy. You *didn't* . . . ?

CROUCH   Hello!

He closes the Front Door behind him.

George turns abruptly and walks swiftly out, to his Study. In the Hall he passes by Crouch.

CROUCH   Excuse me, sir. . . .

GEORGE (*shouts viciously*)   You seem to be taking out the rubbish at any time that suits you!!

Crouch is dumbfounded.

George walks into the Study, leaving the door open, and slumps into his chair.

The Secretary is patient and discreet.

Crouch timidly enters the Study.

CROUCH   I haven't come for the rubbish, sir.

GEORGE   I'm sorry, Mr. Crouch . . . I'm very sorry. I was upset. It's just been the most awful day.

He comforts himself with the tortoise.

CROUCH   I quite understand, sir. I'm upset myself. I just came up to see if there was anything I could do, I knew you'd be upset. . . .

George looks at him.

I got to know him quite well, you know . . . made quite a friend of him.

GEORGE   You knew about it?

CROUCH   I was there, sir. Doing the drinks. It shocked me, I can tell you.

GEORGE   Who killed him?

CROUCH   Well, I wouldn't like to say for certain . . . I mean, I heard a bang, and when I looked, there he was crawling on the floor . . .

George winces.

.... and there was Miss Moore ... well——

GEORGE   Do you realize she's in there now, *eating* him?

CROUCH (*pause*)   You mean—*raw?*

GEORGE (*crossly*)   No, of course not!—*cooked*—with gravy and mashed potatoes.

CROUCH (*pause*)   I thought she was on the mend, sir.

GEORGE   Do you think I'm being too sentimental about the whole thing?

CROUCH (*firmly*)   I do not, sir. I think it's a police matter.

GEORGE   They'd laugh at me. . . . There *was* a policeman here, but he's gone.

CROUCH   Yes, sir, I saw him leave. I thought that would be him. You were wondering, sir, who brought them round.

GEORGE   No. I telephoned them myself.

CROUCH   You're an honest man, sir. In the circumstances I don't mind telling you I also phoned them myself, anonymous.

GEORGE   Did you? . . . Well, it's all right now, he's gone.
   Lot of fuss about nothing. I know things got a bit out of hand but . . . I'm surprised at your puritanism, Mr. Crouch. . . . A little wine, women and song. . . .

CROUCH   Yes, sir. Of course, it was the murder of Professor McFee that was the main thing.

Long pause, George sits perfectly still, and continues to do so, sightless, deaf, while Crouch speaks.

By the way, sir. . . . (*Picking up the tortoise.*) I hope you don't mind my taking the opportunity, but as you know, no pets allowed in the flats—I don't mind turning a blind eye to this little fellow, but I've seen a rabbit around the place of a morning, and it's as

much as my job's worth—I hope you don't mind, sir. . . . (*Pause.*)
Will Miss Moore be . . . leaving, sir?

GEORGE (*blinking awake*)   She's in bed with the doctor. Not
literally, of course.

Small pause. He jumps up and strides into the Bedroom.

*Archie and Dotty are calmly watching the TV. The Big Screen shows us
what they see—the read-back of Dotty's naked body.*

GEORGE   Crouch says—(*he is momentarily taken aback by the fact that
they are watching TV*) Crouch says——

Archie and Dotty go 'Sssssh!' and continue to watch the Screen.

GEORGE (*advancing*)   Crouch says——
(*Then George sees the TV and the naked body on it. He pauses: the
body is familiar to him, perhaps.*) What's going on?

ARCHIE   The dermatograph, you know. All kinds of disturbances
under the skin show up on the surface, if we can learn to read it,
and we——

GEORGE (*abruptly turning off the set, so that the Big Screen goes
blank*)   You must think I'm a bloody fool!

ARCHIE   What do you mean?

GEORGE   Well, everything you do makes it *look* as if you're . . .

Pause.

ARCHIE   Well, what would it have *looked* like if it had *looked* as if I
were making a dermatographical examination?

DOTTY   What's the matter, Georgie?

GEORGE   Dotty . . .

DOTTY   Don't take any notice of Archie—him and his ripe pears!

GEORGE   Crouch says McFee was shot!—here—last night—
He thinks Dorothy did it——

DOTTY I thought Archie did it. *You* didn't do it, did you, Georgie? (*Disappears into Bathroom.*)

GEORGE Crouch says—You can't hide!—Dorothy—it's not a game! Crouch says he *saw*—For God's sake—I don't know what to do——

ARCHIE Crouch says he saw *what*, George?

GEORGE Well, he didn't actually *see* . . .

ARCHIE Quite. We just don't *know.*

GEORGE There are many things I know which are not verifiable but nobody can tell me I don't know them, and I think that I know that something happened to poor Dotty and she somehow killed McFee, as sure as she killed my poor Thumper.

> *George leaves the Bedroom and Archie follows him out. The Bedroom* BLACKS OUT. *They both walk into the Study where Crouch is seated at George's desk, reading the typescript and chuckling!*

CROUCH Saint Sebastian died of fright!—very good! (*To Secretary; surprisingly.*) Of course, the flaw in the argument *is* that even if the first term of his infinitely regressing series is zero rather than infinitesimal, the original problem remains in identifying the *second* term of the series, which however small must be *greater* than zero— you take my point? I grant you he's answered Russell's first point, I grant you that—the smallest proper fraction is zero—*but*——

> *George snatches the paper from behind Crouch and studies it minutely, already talking.*

GEORGE Yes, but you entirely miss *my* point, which is that having established that the first term—that is God—corresponds to zero, there's no need to worry about the second term—it is enough that it *is* the second——Surely you can see that?

CROUCH (*humbly*) I expect you're right, sir. I mean, it's only a hobby with me.

ARCHIE (*coming forward*)   Mr. Crouch!

CROUCH   Oh, good morning, Vice-Chancellor, sir . . .

The situation: Crouch and Archie conversing out of the Study into the Hall. George worrying his script. The Secretary still the observer with pencil and pad ready. Once in the Hall, Archie shuts the Study door.

ARCHIE   I see you're something of a philosopher, Mr. Crouch.

CROUCH   Oh, I wouldn't call it that, sir—I just picked up a bit . . . a bit of reading, a bit of chatting, you know.

ARCHIE   Isn't that the academic life? Whom would you describe as your mentor?

CROUCH   It was the late Professor McFee.

ARCHIE   Really?

CROUCH   Yes, sir, it was a terrible thing, his death. Of course, his whole life was going through a crisis, as he no doubt told you.

ARCHIE   Yes . . . ?

CROUCH   It was the astronauts fighting on the Moon that finally turned him, sir. Henry, he said to me, Henry, I am giving philosophical respectability to a new pragmatism in public life, of which there have been many disturbing examples both here and on the moon. Duncan, I said, Duncan, don't let it get you down, have another can of beer. But he kept harking back to the first Captain Oates, out there in the Antarctic wastes, sacrificing his life to give his companions a slim chance of survival. . . . Henry, he said, what made him do it?—out of the tent and into the jaws of the blizzard. If altruism is a possibility, he said, my argument is up a gum-tree. . . . Duncan, I said, Duncan, don't you worry your head about all that. That astronaut yobbo is good for twenty years hard. Yes, he said, yes *maybe*, but when he comes out, he's going to find he was only twenty years ahead of his time. I have seen the future, Henry, he said; and it's yellow.

ARCHIE (*pause*)   You must have been a close friend of his.

84

From now on, for the following speeches, the Secretary is the only person moving onstage. She gets up. She is going to go for lunch. Perhaps a clock has struck. She comes downstage to make use of the imaginary mirror . . . a grim, tense, unsmiling young woman, staring at the audience.

CROUCH   Ah, well, he'd come by to pick up his girl.

ARCHIE   His girl?

CROUCH   And he was always a bit early and as often as not Professor Moore kept her working a bit late.

ARCHIE   Professor Moore?

CROUCH   So he'd pass the time with me . . . I shall miss our little talks. And of course it's tragic for her. I see she's carrying on, losing herself in her work; it's the only way . . . but after three years of secret betrothal, it takes a certain kind of girl.

ARCHIE   Yes. Why secret?

CROUCH   He made her keep it secret because of his wife.

ARCHIE   Ah. His wife didn't know, of course.

CROUCH   His wife knew about *her*, but *she* didn't know about his wife. He was *terrified* to tell her, poor Duncan. Well, he won't be coming round here any more. Not that he would have done anyway, of course.

ARCHIE   Why's that?

CROUCH   Well obviously, he had to make a clean breast and tell her it was all off—I mean with him going into the monastery.

ARCHIE   Quite.

CROUCH   And now he's dead.

Secretary snaps her handbag shut with a sharp sound and takes her coat out of the cupboard.

85

ARCHIE   A severe blow to Logic, Mr. Crouch.

CROUCH (*nodding*)   It makes no sense to me at all. What do you make of it, sir?

ARCHIE   The truth to us philosophers, Mr. Crouch, is always an interim judgment. We will never even know for certain who did shoot McFee. Unlike mystery novels, life does not guarantee a denouement; and if it came, how would one know whether to believe it?

> *Archie and Crouch move out through the Front Door. The Secretary is also leaving, now wearing her (white) coat—which has a bright splash of blood on its back.*
>
> *George sees the blood as she leaves the Study, and the flat.*
>
> *In the unseen Bedroom, Dotty's record of 'Forget Yesterday' starts to play.*
>
> *George realizes that the blood must have come from the top of the cupboard, i.e. wardrobe. He needs to stand on his desk or chair. He puts Pat, whom he had been holding, down now and climbs up to look into the top of the cupboard; and withdraws from the unseen depths his misfired arrow, on which is impaled Thumper. The music still continues. Holding Thumper up by the arrow, George puts his face against the fur. A single sob. He steps backwards, down . . . CRRRRRUNCH!!!*
>
> *He has stepped, fatally, on Pat. With one foot on the desk and one foot on Pat, George looks down, and then puts up his head and cries out,* 'Dotty! Help! Murder!'
>
> *George falls to the floor. The song continues. The process which originally brought the set into view now goes into reverse. His last sobs are amplified and repeated right into the beginning of the Coda.*

END OF ACT TWO

CODA

The Symposium—in bizarre dream form, Crouch is the Chairman, Archie stands to one side.

Three Ushers (Jumpers) sit in front of Crouch's raised platform. They wear yellow gowns.

Stained glass slides are in at the beginning and stay in. The sobs subside. George lies still.

CROUCH Well, gentlemen, that's approximately two minutes of approximate silence. I think we might proceed with our opening statements—'Man—good, bad or indifferent?'—Sir Archibald.

USHER Call Sir Archibald Jumper!

ECHO Call Sir Archibald Jumper.

George remains prone. Enormous applause, unrealistically cut off, for Archie.

ARCHIE Mr. Crouch, ladies and gentlemen. 'Man—good, bad or indifferent?' Indeed, if moon mad herd instinct, is God dad the inference?—to take another point: If goons in mood, by Gad is sin different or banned good, f'r'instance?—thirdly: out of the ether, random nucleic acid testes or neither universa vice, to name but one—fourthly: If the necessary being isn't, surely mother of invention as Voltaire said, not to mention Darwin different from the origin of the specious—to sum up: Super, both natural and stitious, sexual ergo cogito er go-go sometimes, as Descartes said, and who are we? Thank you. (*Shattering applause. The Ushers hold up score cards: '9.7'—'9.9'—'9.8'.*)

87

ARCHIE   Call the Archbishop of Canterbury.

The cry is taken up by other voices. There is music for the
ARCHBISHOP'*s entrance. He enters, dressed as for a coronation,*
attended by two yellow-garbed Chaplains (Jumpers) who position
themselves downstage, facing the audience. George gets to his feet and
looks at CLEGTHORPE, *who 'blesses' him.*

USHER (*to Archbishop*)   Take the book in your right hand and read
what is on the card.

ARCHBISHOP   Nine.

ARCHIE   My lord, it might save the court's time if I were
to explain now that his Grace has certain doubts about the
existence of God, and does not wish to take the oath, as a matter
of conscience. You are Samuel Clegthorpe, Archbishop of
Canterbury?

ARCHBISHOP   For my sins.

CROUCH   What does he mean by that?

ARCHIE   I think he was hoping for a Cabinet post, my lord.
    . . . Your Grace, we are gathered together to dispute the
goodness, badness or indifference of man. As the senior cleric of
the Church of England, you have no doubt thought deeply about
this.

CLEGTHORPE   Well, until recently, I have been mainly interested
in the birds of the air and the beasts of the field—rooks, badgers,
rabbits—and so on.

ARCHIE   Quite. But I think you are aware that there is great
uncertainty in the land. The ground shifts. The common people to
look to you for guidance.

CLEGTHORPE   Yes. My chaplains had to use tear gas to disperse
them. In my opinion, the Government is going too fast. (*The
Chaplains turn to look at him.*)

ARCHIE   Surely that is a matter best left to the Government?

CLEGTHORPE   They were shouting 'Give us the blood of the lamb. Give us the bread of the body of Christ'——

ARCHIE   That's hardly a rational demand.

CLEGTHORPE   They won't go away! . . . Surely belief in man could find room for man's beliefs . . . ? (*Behind him the Ushers stand up.*)

ARCHIE   Archbishop, the cat has already jumped.

The Chaplains back-flip into the middle of the stage, flanking Clegthorpe now; or cartwheels if back-flips are not possible.

No further questions.

CLEGTHORPE   Well, I'd just like to say—I don't like to see my flock weeping in my garden at Lambeth——

ARCHIE (*sharply*)   My Lord Archbishop, when I was last in Lambeth I saw good strawberries in your garden—I do beseech you send for some.

Ushers and Chaplains take a step.

CLEGTHORPE   Yes, all right, but you must appreciate my position—I mean now that I *am* Archbishop of Canterbury——

ARCHIE   *Will no one rid me of this turbulent priest!*

From each side of the stage, as though catapulted (from trampolines offstage) a Yellow Jumper leaps into the middle of the stage, both Jumpers landing together in front of Clegthorpe, with the first bar of the introduction to 'Sentimental Journey'.

The seven Jumpers (i.e. two Chaplains, three Ushers and the latter two) are now one unit, using the music to choreograph the threat to Clegthorpe.

George watches, moves hesitantly.

This is what happens now, and it ought not to take as long to happen as it does to describe it: The Jumpers and the music together keep the beat. The pattern of men changes and in six separate movements Clegthorpe is moved upstage until he is standing on Crouch's desk as part of a pyramid of Jumpers.

GEORGE Point of order, Mr. Chairman.

CLEGTHORPE Professor—it's not right. George—help.

CROUCH Do you have any questions for this witness, Professor?

GEORGE Er . . . no, I don't think so.

CROUCH Thank you.

The music goes louder.

GEORGE Well, this seems to be a political quarrel. . . . Surely only a proper respect for absolute values . . . universal truths— *philosophy——*

A gunshot. It stops the music, and knocks Clegthorpe out of the pyramid, which disintegrates. When everything is still.

ARCHIE Call Dotty Moore!

Everything comes vividly to life: loud music brings the Jumpers to their feet. The Screen turns to a brilliant starry sky. The music is the introduction to 'Sentimental Journey', and Dotty is to make her entrance on a spangled crescent moon . . . with the Jumpers as Dancers.

JUMPERS (*sing*) Calling Dotty Moore, calling Dotty Moore, call Dotty Moore.

DOTTY (*sings*) Did I hear you call, will you tell me why?
  Am I dreaming, is this really me?
  Show me where to stand, and I'll tell you my Philosophy.

  Here is my consistent proposition,
  Two and two make roughly four—

Gentlemen, that is my position,
Yours sincerely, Dorothy Moore.

As for man, I got my reservations,
Going by experience
Some ain't bad and some are revelations,
Never met indifference.

Heaven, how can I believe in heaven?
Just a lying rhyme for seven!
Scored for violins on multi-track
That takes me back
To happy days when I knew how to make it
I knew how to hold a tune
Till the night they had to go and break it——

GEORGE (*shouts*)   *Stop!!*

Everything freezes.

A remarkable number of apparently intelligent people are baffled
by the fact that a different group of apparently intelligent people
profess to a knowledge of God when common sense tells *them*—
the first group of apparently intelligent people—that knowledge
is only a possibility in matters that can be demonstrated to be true
or false, such as that the Bristol train leaves from Paddington. And
yet these same apparently intelligent people, who in extreme cases
will not even admit that the Bristol train left from Paddington
yesterday—which might be a malicious report or a collective
trick of memory—nor that it will leave from there tomorrow—
for nothing is certain—and will only agree that it did so today if
they were actually there when it left—and even then only on the
understanding that all the observable phenomena associated with
the train leaving Paddington could equally well be accounted
for by Paddington leaving the train—these same people will,
nevertheless, and without any sense of inconsistency, claim to
know that life is better than death, that love is better than hate,
and that the light shining through the east window of their

bloody gymnasium is more beautiful than a rotting corpse!—In evidence of which I ask you, gentlemen of the jury, to consider the testimony of such witnesses as Zeno Evil, St. Thomas Augustine, Jesus Moore and my late friend the late Herr Thumper who was as innocent as a rainbow . . .

ARCHIE   Do not despair—many are happy much of the time; more eat than starve, more are healthy than sick, more curable than dying; not so many dying as dead; and one of the thieves was saved. Hell's bells and all's well—half the world is at peace with itself, and so is the other half; vast areas are unpolluted; millions of children grow up without suffering deprivation, and millions, while deprived, grow up without suffering cruelties, and millions, while deprived and cruelly treated, none the less grow up. No laughter is sad and many tears are joyful. At the graveside the undertaker doffs his top hat and impregnates the prettiest mourner. Wham, bam, thank you Sam. (*The light has reduced to a spot on Dotty.*)

DOTTY (*sings without music*)   Goodbye spoony Juney Moon.

BLACKOUT

FORGET YESTERDAY

If you don't love me this morning
Don't break the news too soon;
Can't keep the daylight from dawning,
Can't face the afternoon.
But save it baby I'll get by
Tell me under a starry sky
Just like you found me
Want you to leave me
Below a lover's moon.
Call it a day but wait for the night
Don't go away the sun is still high
I'll drink to you in moonshine tonight
Tell me I'm through I'll find someone new
You won't see me cry.

Don't have to give me the lowdown,
Call off the honeymoon
You paid the piper but slow down,
Take time to call the tune.
Need time 'til all my tears have dried
Catch me when I'm all starry eyed.
Just like you found me
Want you to leave me
Below a lover's moon.
Call it a day, it's nearly tonight
Help me to keep tomorrow at bay
I'll dream of you, pretend it's all right,
Maybe it's true
Tomorrow is new
Forget yesterday.